Standard Grade | General | Credit

English

First exam published in 2001.
Published by Leckie & Leckie, 8 Whitehill Terrace, St. Andrews, Scotland KY16 8RN tel: 01334 475656 fax: 01334 477392
enquiries@leckieandleckie.co.uk www.leckieandleckie.co.uk

ISBN 1-84372-298-4

A CIP Catalogue record for this book is available from the British Library.

Printed in Scotland by Scotprint.

Leckie & Leckie is a division of Granada Learning Limited, part of ITV plc.

Acknowledgements

Leckie & Leckie is grateful to the copyright holders, as credited at the back of the book, for permission to use their material. Every effort has been made to trace the copyright holders and to obtain their permission for the use of copyright material. Leckie & Leckie will gladly receive information enabling them to rectify any error or omission in subsequent editions.

[BLANK PAGE]

G

0860/403

NATIONAL
QUALIFICATIONS
2001

MONDAY, 14 MAY
1.00 PM – 1.50 PM

ENGLISH
STANDARD GRADE
General Level
Reading
Text

Read carefully the passage overleaf. It will help if you read it twice. When you have done so, answer the questions. Use the spaces provided in the Question/Answer booklet.

SCOTTISH
QUALIFICATIONS
AUTHORITY

©

The Appeal of

1 All the junk in Scotland meets your befuddled gaze: thousands of unwanted gifts, the "wee something" for Christmas and the "I saw this and thought of you" for your birthday (how you wish they hadn't); then there are the holiday souvenirs. In short, all the stuff with which we tend to clutter our lives and our cupboards has somehow ended up in one place, awkwardly arranged on a vast number of folding tables.

2 Behind them, all kinds of people are perched on the tailgates of a variety of vehicles. Is this some bizarre store for recycled rubbish? Well, in a way it is. In other words, you have found yourself in the middle of your first car boot sale. They can be found most weekends in summer, and sometimes in winter too, in villages, towns and cities throughout the country. Sometimes they are held on an occasional basis—a charity or other organisation will hire a hall or a school playground, advertise in the local press and rent out pitches at £5 or £10 for the day. Other sales are held every Saturday or Sunday on more permanent sites.

3 Women seem to outnumber men behind the essential tables: although men often come to help to set up, they retire shyly for most of the day and return in the late afternoon to pack up the left-overs. Curiously enough, there are as many male customers as female: all human life wanders by.

4 There goes a plump medallion man who will tell you—his unhappily captive audience—a succession of unfunny and wildly politically incorrect jokes at which you will laugh, lamely, and hope he goes away.

5 There goes a succession of polite elderly gentlemen, clean and smart in their car coats; they will go off happily clutching boxes of your ancient gardening tools to which their wives will most surely object, but who are you to spoil their fun?

6 There is, just occasionally, a serious side to all this, which may affect the buyer rather than the genuine seller. Car boot sales can provide a certain amount of cover for less honest traders and it is as well to bear this in mind if you are offered a more than average bargain. Where, for instance, did those big canisters of cleaning fluid designated "Janitorial Supplies" originate? And what about those suspiciously home-made looking video cassettes of all the latest movies? Trading Standards Officers sometimes visit boot sales to keep a lookout for fakes. Police

Never underestimate what will sell. Old console games o
market for a

occasionally find stolen goods lurking among the junk. Customs and Excise may be investigating those suspiciously cheap cigarettes and Environmental Health Officers may even be wondering whether that delicious home-made tablet has been concocted with due regard to public health.

7 But on the whole, say the police, they have little trouble with car boot sales. Most are legitimate and harmless: ordinary punters offloading bric-a-brac onto other ordinary punters. To a Martian hovering up there we must all look like nothing so much as a colony of ants, struggling to carry off various large and cumbersome objects, a table here, a suitcase there . . .

8 So if you fancy trying a boot sale, just for the fun of it, here are a few ground rules for participating in this most rewarding game.

9 Go as a buyer first, if you can. Have a good look around. Some pitches are better than others. Some are closer to the loos. Some are on windy corners and some may be right next to the little roundabout that plays the same four-bar tune all day long.

10 Go early, if you are selling. Many car boot sales that advertise an opening time of 10 am are being set up by seven or eight in the morning.

Pa

Car Boot Sales

deos will disappear as if by magic and there is a ready
nds of gadgets.

11   Beware of the antique dealers. They will surround your table at this early hour like wild dogs around a carcase, fingering your Aunty Annie's floral teapot with its dripping spout and trying to decide if they are getting the bargain of the century at £1·50 including chipped lid.   Remember the Antiques Roadshow. Remember that daft little pottery owl that fetched thousands.

12   Invest in a cheap wallpapering table. You can sell out of the boot of your car, but if you have as much junk to get rid of as most of us do, you will need more space than the average hatchback can supply. Take a secure container for your money—preferably a money belt so that you can keep your takings safely about your person.   Don't leave handbags lying around; car boot sales are hunting grounds for purse snatchers. By the same token it's wise to take a friend. Then you have someone to mind the stall while you take time out to browse around the neighbouring stalls.

13   Don't sell old electrical goods: they can be dangerous, and you can be in trouble with the law for doing so.

14   Take lots of food and drink with you: sandwiches, chocolate bars, flasks of tea and coffee, cans of soft drinks. You will be amazed at how hungry and thirsty you will get standing around all day and there is little point in blowing your takings on hamburgers although the smell will certainly drive you wild. Wear comfortable shoes and remember to take warm clothes, even in summer.   Remember to plan for rain.   This is Scotland after all, and you will probably get cold and wet.

15   Don't overprice your goods, but never underestimate what will sell either. The truth is that people will buy almost anything if the price is right.   Old Playstation games, or genuine second-hand videos, will disappear as if by magic.   Even more surprisingly, so will large, rickety (and empty) wooden boxes, elderly baseball caps that were given free with something ten years ago, shabby plastic dinosaurs that have been in many an imaginary battle and a pile of kitchen gadgets such as the tattie peeling machine that always took ages to wash afterwards, the expensive plastic containers with ill-fitting lids and the pancake mixer that liberally sprinkled you with batter every time you tried to use it. Just lay it out and somebody will come along wanting to buy it.

16   Above all, don't expect to make any fortunes. What you will do is recycle a truly astonishing amount of junk, give an amazing amount of pleasure to all kinds of people, observe all human life wandering past your table, and come home with a modest profit. That's if you can stop yourself from filling your car boot with other people's junk before you go home.

17   After all there's a little collection of pressed glass over there that is so irresistible, and the old hand-knitted Shetland shawl that nobody seems to have spotted, and isn't that a genuine stone hot-water bottle lurking among the rubbish . . . ?

Adapted from an article in "The Scotsman" by Catherine Czerkawska.

[END OF PASSAGE]

wo

[BLANK PAGE]

FOR OFFICIAL USE

G

Total Mark

0860/404

NATIONAL
QUALIFICATIONS
2001

MONDAY, 14 MAY
1.00 PM – 1.50 PM

ENGLISH
STANDARD GRADE
General Level
Reading
Questions

Fill in these boxes and read what is printed below.

Full name of centre

Town

Forename(s)

Surname

Date of birth
Day Month Year   Scottish candidate number   Number of seat

**NB Before leaving the examination room you must give this booklet to the invigilator.
If you do not, you may lose all the marks for this paper.**

SCOTTISH
QUALIFICATIONS
AUTHORITY

QUESTIONS

Write your answers in the spaces provided.

Look at Paragraphs 1 and 2.

1. "All the junk in Scotland meets your befuddled gaze"

   How does the writer continue the idea of "junk" in the first two paragraphs?

   _____

   _____

   2
   1
   0

2. **Write down an expression** from Paragraph 2 which shows that the writer thinks this "junk" makes a **strange collection**.

   _____

   2
   1
   0

3. Explain the **differences** between the two types of car boot sale described in Paragraph 2.

   (i) _____

   _____

   2
   1
   0

   (ii) _____

   _____

   2
   1
   0

Look at Paragraphs 3 to 5.

4. (a) When it comes to selling, women "seem to outnumber men".

   Write down the expression the writer uses to suggest why the men don't do the selling.

   _____

   _____

   2
   0

   (b) When it comes to buying, there are "as many male customers as female".

   What is the writer's reaction to this? Answer in your own words.

   _____

   2
   0

5. (*a*) The writer gives two examples of "human life" wandering by.
In your own words, explain as fully as you can why the writer:

(i) disapproves of the "plump medallion man" _____

_____

_____

2
1
0

(ii) might sympathise with the "succession of polite elderly gentlemen".

_____

_____

2
1
0

(*b*) Explain fully what the writer gains by using the expression "There goes . . ." to introduce these two examples.

_____

_____

2
1
0

Look at Paragraphs 6 and 7.

6. Explain **in your own words** what the writer means by the "serious side" of car boot sales.

_____

_____

2
1
0

7. (*a*) What do each of the following organisations look for at car boot sales?

(i) Trading Standards _____

(ii) Police _____

2
1
0

(iii) Customs and Excise _____

(*b*) Explain what concerns the Environmental Health Officers might have about any food on sale.

_____

_____

2
1
0

8. **Write down** an expression which shows that there are very few concerns about the "serious side" of car boot sales.

_____

2
0

Look at Paragraphs 8 to 14.

9. In Paragraph 8 the writer introduces the idea of giving practical advice.

How does the sentence construction at the beginning of Paragraphs 9 to 14 help to show this?

_____

2
0

10. (a) **Write down** the simile or comparison which describes how the antique dealers behave.

_____

2
0

(b) Explain what is appropriate about this comparison.

_____

2
1
0

11. From Paragraph 12, **explain in your own words** why:

(a) you should "invest in a cheap wallpapering table".

_____

_____

2
1
0

(b) you would be "wise to take a friend".

_____

_____

2
1
0

Look at Paragraph 15.

12. ". . . people will buy almost anything . . ."

The writer gives several examples to prove this statement.

Choose any **two** (APART FROM GAMES AND VIDEOS).

In each case explain why the writer thinks it is surprising that anyone should buy them.

(i) _____   2
                                                         1
_____   0

(ii) _____   2
                                                         1
_____   0

Look at Paragraphs 16 and 17.

13. The writer believes several benefits can be gained from car boot sales. **In your own words** describe two of them.

(i) _____   2
                                                         1
(ii) _____   0

14. What do you think the writer is suggesting by her descriptions of the items in Paragraph 17?   2
                                                         1
_____   0

15. Why does the writer use ellipsis (. . .) at the end of the final sentence?
                                                         2
_____   0

Think about the passage as a whole.

16. Look at the photograph which accompanies the article.

Explain how it shows examples of the following:

(i) the writer's advice being taken _____

_____

(ii) the writer's advice being ignored _____   2
                                                               1
_____   0

[Turn over for Question 17 on *Page six*

17. Tick (✓) **one** of the following expressions which you think **best** describes the writer's purpose in this article.

Explain your choice by detailed reference to the text.

to provide information ☐   to entertain ☐

to be thought-provoking ☐

_____

_____

_____

_____

2
1
0

[END OF QUESTION PAPER]

2001 Reading | Credit

[BLANK PAGE]

C

0860/405

NATIONAL QUALIFICATIONS 2001	MONDAY, 14 MAY 2.30 PM – 3.20 PM	ENGLISH STANDARD GRADE Credit Level Reading Text

Read carefully the passage overleaf. It will help if you read it twice. When you have done so, answer the questions. Use the spaces provided in the Question/Answer booklet.

SCOTTISH QUALIFICATIONS AUTHORITY

In this extract the narrator reflects on the first visit of an aunt and cousin.

1   They didn't come to England till 1962. It was the "n"-th year of preparations for a visit that always, in the end, failed to happen.

2   I'd just arrived home for autumn half-term and at first I didn't believe what I was told—that their plane had touched down at the airport—and I wasn't convinced till I saw for myself the black Humber Hawk taxi come swinging up the drive, axles creaking, carrying its two passengers in the back, one swathed in furs.

3   "It's your cousin," my mother told me unnecessarily, nervous beside me on the top step as we made a little reception committee with my father for our guests none of us had ever seen.

4   The driver opened the back door of the taxi and my "aunt", as we referred to her—really my mother's aunt's daughter—divested herself of the travelling rugs. She hazarded a foot out on to the gravel—in a pointy crocodile shoe—as if she were testing the atmosphere. She emerged dressed in a waisted black cashmere overcoat with a fur collar and strange scalloped black kid-skin gloves like hawking gauntlets.

5   I saw my mother noting again the black stiletto-heeled shoes with their red piping. The face we'd never seen was hidden under a broad-brimmed black felt hat, which I felt none of the women *we* knew in our closed circle would have had the courage to put on their heads.

6   "Hi!" my aunt greeted us in a surprisingly light, sprightly voice, unpinning the furs across her shoulders.

7   A shadow moved behind her in the car. Behind them both the driver was lifting half a dozen assorted white suitcases out of the boot. My mother drew in her breath.

8   "It's so cold!" my aunt called to us from under her hat. "Brr, I can't take it like this!"

9   Then she smiled—at the three of us, each in turn—quite charmingly.

10   My mother relaxed, realising our guest was only being eccentric, not insulting.

11   "Well I hope you'll be warm *here*," my mother told her by way of introduction, with just a little "tone" in her voice.

12   I could see better now. Beneath her discreetly black coat my aunt had very long, slender, shapely legs. Behind her, her son—my cousin Walter—ventured unsurely into the hall.

13   "Unfortunately," my mother addressed the face under the hat, "you've come at the very coldest season."

14   "Oh, I know I'll be very warm here, I can tell already," my aunt assured her with another toothpaste advertisement smile, throwing her furs on to a chair like a film star. "Very comfortable. I've so wanted to see you all, you can't imagine."

15   My mother smiled—cautiously—and my father closed the door.

16   "Do come and have some tea, both of you," he said.

17   He was forever at a loss with guests to Oakdene, my father: now for some reason a smile was starting to break on his reserved banker's "business" face my mother and I were so used to living with.

18   I examined my cousin surreptitiously while I helped my father carry the cases to the foot of the staircase—while *he* just stood there, doing nothing. He was odd-looking, I saw. He had a triangular-shaped face with a bony chin, and he was bloodlessly, alarmingly pale. He stood with his shoulders hunched; very arched eyebrows and flat ears set close against his head added to the pixie-ness of his appearance. What made me think him odder still was his not seeming to match at all with his elegant (and, from what I could see, pretty) mother. (How ugly must his father be, I wondered, to correct the balance of heredity?) He was several inches shorter than I was, although I knew we were the same age (eleven, if the year was 1962). His height—or his lack of height—was another disappointment, and also his thinness. I'd expected he would look stolid, and assertive, and the very picture of glowing health. Instead the eyes in his pale face flitted among us, like a prying spinster's, missing nothing.

19   "Did you have a nice flight?" my mother asked, with controlled politeness. "I can't remember where . . ."

20   "Oh, we've been everywhere! Everywhere!" my aunt explained, pausing at the hatstand to remove her wide-brimmed hat. She seemed to take off twenty years with it and suddenly I felt they were a generation apart, she and my mother. My aunt pulled at her hair—becomingly blonde (dyed, I think it must have been) and smartly cut—with the tips of her fingers. In her black crocodile shoes and with her black lizard bag and the long kid gloves tucked into the pockets of her coat, she looked very expensive. I was utterly fascinated.

21   "Paris. Como. Rome." She crossed them off on those creamed, manicured fingers with their scarlet nails. (She was making little perfume trails whenever she moved.) "Where else, now? Antibes, of course. And we saw a little bit of Switzerland. That *was* cold!"

22   She walked ahead of us into the sitting-room and made for the fireplace and the crackling log fire.

23   "Capri. That was just heaven. And Naples, of course."

24   My mother watched her from the hall. "Of course," she repeated, just to herself, under her breath.

25   Their visit to us was bad timing. We were having a very cold snap, and in another week—when our guests would have gone—it would be November, then December after that, with Christmas fir trees for sale in the village shops. We were to be their last stop before they flew home. I suppose we were a family obligation. Or—were we really something else, a different kind of invitation to their travellers' curiosity . . . ?

26   In our sitting-room my aunt seemed very exotic, and rather theatrical: not at all like my staid "county" mother with her scrubbed grouse-moor complexion. For "housewives", how unalike they seemed! On a scale of prettiness my aunt might have scored seven marks out of ten: she certainly "made the most of what she had"—as my mother would say of certain women she didn't quite approve of, because (another of her expressions) they "tried too hard".

[Turn over

27   When my aunt took off her coat she was wearing a canary silk suit underneath, and my mother looked most uncomfortable in the other big wing-chair, pulling her tweed skirt over her knees and tugging at the pearls round her throat. My cousin Walter sat, not where he was invited to, but on a hard-bottomed shield-back chair from where he could observe all our different posturings with his range of vision clear and unimpeded.

28   My aunt burst the seal on a pack of cigarettes and leaned forward in her chair to catch the flame from my father's lighter. I saw my mother taking a suddenly critical view of the situation. Her face was set in a way I wasn't unfamiliar with.

29   "You'll have some tea, Stella?"

30   My aunt nodded through the thick blue fog of cigarette smoke. I noticed how speedily her eyes were racing round our sitting-room, as Walter's had done earlier, recording our possessions.

31   Like my mother I was already starting to feel not at all at my ease: almost—silly to say—like a stranger here in my own home.

Adapted from a short story by Ronald Frame

[END OF PASSAGE]

FOR OFFICIAL USE

C

Total Mark

0860/406

NATIONAL QUALIFICATIONS 2001

MONDAY, 14 MAY 2.30 PM – 3.20 PM

ENGLISH STANDARD GRADE
Credit Level
Reading
Questions

Fill in these boxes and read what is printed below.

Full name of centre

Town

Forename(s)

Surname

Date of birth
Day Month Year

Scottish candidate number

Number of seat

NB Before leaving the examination room you must give this booklet to the invigilator. If you do not, you may lose all the marks for this paper.

SCOTTISH
QUALIFICATIONS
AUTHORITY

QUESTIONS

Write your answers in the spaces provided.

Look at Paragraphs 1 to 3.

1. **In your own words,** explain fully why the narrator at first didn't believe that "their plane had touched down at the airport".

_____

_____

2
1
0

2. What finally convinced him it was true?

_____

_____

2
1
0

3. (*a*) Why was the narrator's mother "nervous"?

_____

_____

2
1
0

   (*b*) What evidence is there of her nervousness?

_____

2
0

Look at Paragraphs 4 and 5.

4. (*a*) What impression of the aunt do you get from the writer's choice of the words "divested", "hazarded" and "emerged" to describe her movements?

_____

2
0

   (*b*) What is added to this impression by his description of what she was wearing?

_____

2
0

5. What is the function of the dashes (—) used in Paragraph 4?

_____

2
0

Look at Paragraphs 6 to 15.

6. "My mother drew in her breath." (Paragraph 7)

   (*a*) What does this tell you about her feelings?

   _____

   2
   0

   (*b*) What caused her to react this way?

   _____

   _____

   2
   1
   0

7. Explain **in your own words** why the mother, in welcoming the aunt, spoke with just a little "tone" in her voice.

   _____

   _____

   2
   1
   0

8. (*a*) What impression of cousin Walter is given in Paragraph 12?

   _____

   2
   0

   (*b*) How does the writer prepare us for this image of Walter earlier in this section?

   _____

   _____

   2
   1
   0

Look at Paragraphs 16 to 18.

9. Explain **in your own words**:

   (*a*) in what **two** ways the father reacted to the guests;

   _____

   _____

   2
   1
   0

   (*b*) why in each case this was unusual.

   _____

   _____

   2
   1
   0

[Turn over

10. Quote an expression which shows that the narrator tried to find out about his cousin in a secretive way.

_____

2
0

11. "He was odd-looking . . ."

Explain **in your own words** what the narrator seemed to think was the strangest thing about his cousin.

_____

_____

2
1
0

12. What does the last sentence of Paragraph 18 tell us about Walter's character?

_____

2
0

Look at Paragraphs 19 to 24.

13. Using your own words, explain why the narrator gave so many details about his aunt.

_____

_____

2
1
0

14. " 'Of course,' she repeated, just to herself, under her breath."

What does this suggest the mother thought of the aunt's tales of travel?

_____

2
0

Look at Paragraph 25.

15. According to the narrator, what were the **two** possible reasons for the relatives' visits? **Answer in your own words**.

(i) _____

_____

2
1
0

(ii) _____

_____

2
1
0

Look at Paragraphs 26 to 31.

16. "... how unalike they seemed!"

Give details of **two** obvious contrasts between the aunt and the mother.

(i) _____

_____

2
0

(ii) _____

_____

2
0

17. What does the writer's use of the word "posturings" (Paragraph 27) tell you about the behaviour of the people in the room?

_____

_____

2
0

Think about the passage as a whole.

18. Why do you think the writer makes frequent use of brackets throughout the passage?

_____

_____

2
0

19. The narrator began to feel "like a stranger" in his own home. (Paragraph 31)

By close reference to the text, show how his feelings towards his aunt changed.

_____

_____

_____

2
1
0

[END OF QUESTION PAPER]

[BLANK PAGE]

2002 Reading | General

[BLANK PAGE]

G

0860/403

NATIONAL
QUALIFICATIONS
2002

TUESDAY, 7 MAY
1.00 PM – 1.50 PM

ENGLISH
STANDARD
GRADE
General Level
Reading

Read carefully the passage overleaf. It will help if you read it twice. When you have done so, answer the questions. Use the spaces provided in the Question/Answer booklet.

SCOTTISH
QUALIFICATIONS
AUTHORITY

©

1   The kettle switched itself off the boil with a sharp click. The young man filled the teapot with the steaming water and dropped in a teabag to add to the one already there. He sat the full pot on the formica-topped breakfast bar and made a silly face at his five-year-old daughter who was perched on a stool slowly getting through a bowl of milky porridge. Hearing his wife coming down the stairs from the bathroom he began to refill her mug but instead of entering the bright warm kitchen she lingered in the hall. He could hear her pulling on her heavy coat. She came in saying she had no time, she'd be late for her lift, her heels clattering on the tiled floor. She kissed goodbye to daughter and husband then was off in a whirl of newly-applied perfume and the swish of her clothes and the front door slamming.

2   He sat down on his stool and poured himself another mug of tea. He asked the child how she was doing, was the porridge too hot? She told him gravely that it was OK and went on making a show of blowing on each hot spoonful as she had been shown.

3   He picked up the newspaper that was lying folded open at the Situations Vacant pages. One advert was targeted in a ring of red felt-tip pen. The introduction was in big bold italics: *"This time last year I was made redundant. Now I own a £150,000 house, drive a BMW and holiday in Bali. If you . . ."* He opened out the paper and refolded it to the front page to check the headlines. The date he knew already but there it was: exactly one year he had been out of work.

4   Father and daughter chatted brightly as they strolled hand in hand down Allison Street heading for school. She was a talkative child and he would egg her on in her prattle for his own amusement. It was now well into the rush hour: traffic gushed by or fretted at red lights and urgent pedestrians commanded the pavements and crossings. It was bitter cold. He looked down at the girl to reassure himself that she was warmly enough dressed, but there was no need; he was well used to getting her ready. Her round reddened face was the only prey to the cold air and she beamed up at him, quite content.

5   At the last corner before the school's street they both halted in an accustomed way and he squatted down to give her a kiss. She didn't mind the ritual but not outside the gates: her pals might see and that would be too embarrassing. He tugged her knitted hat a little further down her forehead and tucked in a couple of strands of her long reddish hair. They could hear the kids' voices laughing and shouting from the playground. They waved cheerio at the gate and he stood watching until she was inside and with her friends, then he turned away. He was vaguely aware of one or two mothers doing likewise and one or two car doors slamming. With both gloveless hands shoved into the pockets of his cream-coloured raincoat he made for home. Behind him the bell began to sound above and through the high excited voices.

*   *   *   *   *

6   He finished writing the letter and signed his name with a brisk underline, printing it in brackets below, just in case. Picking up the CV from the coffee table he glanced over the familiar details of his education and career. It looked good, he thought, organised, businesslike. His wife had managed to get a couple of dozen of them run off on her word processor at the office. It was the contents that struck him as pointless. What use was it to anyone to know what he had done at school? It was the grown man, someone with work experience, who was on offer, not the schoolboy. Not the kid who'd scuffed along, neither brilliant nor stupid, not the football-daft apprentice smoker who'd put his name to those long-forgotten exam papers then sauntered out carefree into the world. Well, maybe not carefree: he could still

remember some of the burdens and terrors of adolescence that he'd laugh at now. Then there was his five years of selling for the one firm. No problem there; those were good years. Their fruits were holidays abroad, marriage, the house, the baby. Plain sailing until the company had gone bust. Now he was no longer young and upwardly mobile. Not even horizontally mobile: stopped, stuck.

7   Referees. He always wanted to write the name of a football referee but didn't. What did people expect to hear from the names he always supplied—"Don't touch this character, he's a definite no-user"? It was just wee games, this form-filling. He believed it was the interview that would count, if only he could land one.

8   He arranged the letter and CV together, tapping sides and tails until there was no overlap, then folded them in half and in half again. The envelope was ready, briskly typed by his wife on the old manual machine she used for home typing jobs. As he made ready to lick the stamp he stopped suddenly. He'd done it again, folding the sheets in half twice. That was clumsy, unprofessional-looking. The way she'd shown him was much better: folding one third then another so that you only had two folds instead of three. Gingerly, he tried to reopen the envelope but it was stuck fast and the flap ripped jaggedly. He'd have to type another one himself in his laborious two-fingered style. His first go had two mistakes and so he typed another one, slowly, making sure he got everything right.

*   *   *   *   *

9   He kept walking, on past the pillar-box at the corner of their street. That one was definitely unlucky: nothing he had ever posted there had brought good fortune. No, he would carry on to Victoria Road whose offices and air of industry made it feel a more hopeful point of departure. As he reached the main thoroughfare he saw a mail van pull up at the postbox he was heading for and he quickened his pace. He watched the grey-uniformed driver jump down and unlock the red door; he broke into a run. The pillar-box yielded a bulky flow of mail to the driver's hand combing it into his big shapeless bag. The young man handed over his letter with a half-smile although his heart had sunk. One letter in all that flow of paper. And how many were job applications piled randomly, meaninglessly on top of one another? His own would soon be lost in that anonymous crowd. It seemed to him now more than ever like buying a raffle ticket, like doing the football coupon every week. What chance had you got?

10   But it was easy standing here to recall the bustle of business life. It came to him how much he wanted it, that activity. It was more than just something you did to make money: it was the only life he knew and he was missing out on it, standing on the sidelines like a face in the crowd at a football game. If it wasn't for the child, he thought, he wouldn't have the will to keep on trying. He checked his watch: the kids would soon be coming out.

*   *   *   *   *

11   He waited at their corner, hands deep in pockets, his shoulder to the dirty grey sandstone wall. The bell was ringing and he could hear the children streaming out into the playground. When she spotted him she broke into a trot and he retreated round the corner a little to swoop suddenly with a mock roar, bearing her laughing wildly up into his arms. As he set her down he asked quite formally what kind of morning she'd had. She began to speak, and her enthusiasm breathed upwards into his smiling face and beyond in the chill air.

Adapted from the short story "Application" by Michael Munro

[*END OF PASSAGE*]

FOR OFFICIAL USE

G

Total
Mark

0860/404

NATIONAL
QUALIFICATIONS
2002

TUESDAY, 7 MAY
1.00 PM – 1.50 PM

**ENGLISH
STANDARD
GRADE**
General Level
Reading
Questions

Fill in these boxes and read what is printed below.

Full name of centre

Town

Forename(s)

Surname

Date of birth
Day Month Year   Scottish candidate number   Number of seat

**NB Before leaving the examination room you must give this booklet to the invigilator.
If you do not, you may lose all the marks for this paper.**

SCOTTISH
QUALIFICATIONS
AUTHORITY

MCB 0860/404 6/70170

©

QUESTIONS

Write your answers in the spaces provided.

Look at Paragraphs 1 to 3.

1. Why did the young man have time to make breakfast for his wife and daughter?

   _____   2 ■

2. From the last sentence in Paragraph 1, **write down two separate words** which suggest his wife was in a hurry.

   2 1

3. (a) In Paragraph 1, why is "**perched**" a particularly suitable word to describe how the five-year-old girl sat on her stool?

   _____

   _____   2 1

   (b) Give **two** pieces of evidence to show that the daughter treated the business of eating her breakfast seriously.

   (i) _____

   _____   2 1

   (ii) _____

   _____   2 1

4. Why do you think one advert in the newspaper was "targeted in a ring of red felt-tip pen" (Paragraph 3)?

   _____

   _____   2 1

Marks

Look at Paragraphs 4 and 5.

5. What did the young man enjoy about the walk to school with his daughter? **Answer in your own words.**

_____

_____ | 2 | 1 | 0 |

6. The writer uses a colon (:) in Paragraph 4 (after "rush hour") and in Paragraph 5 (after "outside the gates").

Tick (✓) the box to show which you think is the correct reason for its use in each case. | 2 | 1 | 0 |

	Paragraph 4	*Paragraph 5*
To introduce a quotation		
To elaborate on an idea		
To introduce an explanation		

7. Write down **two** examples of **separate words** the writer has used to convey the idea of "rush hour".

| 2 | 1 | 0 |

8. "It was bitter cold." (Paragraph 4)

Explain clearly how later in Paragraph 4 the writer makes the cold air seem alive.

_____

_____ | 2 | 1 | 0 |

[Turn over

PAGE
TOTAL

Mar

9. (a) Why is the father's kiss described as a "ritual" (Paragraph 5)?

_____

_____ 2 1

(b) Which expression earlier in Paragraph 5 helps you to understand the meaning of "ritual"?

_____ 2 ■

10. ". . . but not outside the gates . . ." (Paragraph 5)

Using your own words as far as possible, explain why the daughter made this condition.

_____

_____ 2 1

Look at Paragraphs 6 and 7.

11. (a) What did the man think "looked good" about his CV?

_____

_____ 2 ■

(b) What **two** things about "this form-filling" did he think were "pointless"?
In each case explain **why** he thought so.

(i) _____

_____ 2 1

(ii) _____

_____ 2 1

Marks

Look at Paragraph 8.

12. (*a*) Why did the man not put the stamp on the envelope?

_____

_____ 2 1 0

(*b*) "Gingerly, he tried to reopen . . . flap ripped jaggedly."

How does the structure of this sentence emphasise the man's care in reopening the envelope?

_____

_____ 2 1 0

(*c*) **Write down** the **two** expressions the writer uses in this paragraph to show the contrast between the man's typing skills and his wife's. 2 1 0

(i) _____

(ii) _____

Look at Paragraphs 9 and 10.

13. Explain clearly why the man chose to post his letter in Victoria Road.

_____

_____

_____ 2 1 0

14. Explain clearly why "his heart had sunk" (Paragraph 9) when he handed over his letter.

_____

_____ 2 1 0

[Turn over for Questions 15 to 17 on *Page six*

PAGE
TOTAL

Ma

15. " . . . standing on the sidelines like a face in the crowd at a football game."
(Paragraph 10)

Explain how effective you find this simile.

_____

_____   2

Think about the passage as a whole.

16. Throughout the passage, the man is shown to be thoughtful and caring about his daughter.

What evidence is there of this:

(*a*) in Paragraph 11?   2

   (i) _____

   (ii) _____

(*b*) elsewhere in the passage?   2

   (i) _____

   (ii) _____

17. Overall, do you feel the story conveys a sense of **hope**, or of **despair**?

Tick (✓) the box to indicate your choice.

Hope	
Despair	

Justify your choice by detailed reference to the text.

_____

_____

_____

_____   2

[END OF QUESTION PAPER]

PA
TO

[BLANK PAGE]

C

0860/405

NATIONAL
QUALIFICATIONS
2002

TUESDAY, 7 MAY
2.30 PM – 3.20 PM

**ENGLISH
STANDARD GRADE**
Credit Level
Reading
Text

Read carefully the passage overleaf. It will help if you read it twice. When you have done so, answer the questions. Use the spaces provided in the Question/Answer booklet.

SCOTTISH
QUALIFICATIONS
AUTHORITY

©

This passage concerns a store detective's encounter with an unusual shoplifter.

1   Sometimes on dark winter mornings he watched them before the doors were opened: pressing their hands and faces against the glass, a plague of moths wanting in to the light. But you couldn't look at them like that, as an invading swarm. To do the job – which was under threat anyway because of security guards and surveillance cameras – you had to get in among them, make yourself invisible. You had to blend in, pretend to be one of them, but you also had to observe them, you had to see the hand slipping the "Game Boy" into the sleeve. Kids wore such loose clothes nowadays, baggy jeans and jogging tops two sizes too big for them. It was the fashion, but it meant they could hide their plunder easily. You had to watch the well-dressed gentlemen as well – the Crombie coat and the briefcase could conceal a fortune in luxury items. When it came down to it, you were a spy.

2   He was in the food hall and they were rushing around him. He picked up a wire basket and strolled through the vegetables, doing his best to look interested in a packet of Continental Salad, washed and ready to use. It was easy to stop taking anything in and let the shopping and the shoplifting happen around you, a blur, an organism, an animal called The Public. The Public was all over the shop: poking its nose into everything; trying on the clean new underwear; squirting the testers on its chin, on its wrists, behind its ears; wriggling its fingers into the gloves; squeezing its warm, damp feet into stiff, new shoes; tinkering with the computers; thumbing the avocados.

3   He was watching a grey-haired lady dressed in a sagging blue raincoat, probably in her sixties, doing exactly that. The clear blue eyes, magnified by thick lenses, looked permanently shocked. A disappointed mouth, darkened by a plum-coloured lipstick, floundered in a tight net of wrinkles. There was something in her movements that was very tense, yet she moved slowly, as if she had been stunned by some very bad news.

4   She put down the avocados – three of them, packaged in polythene – as if she'd just realised what they were and didn't need them. He followed her as she made her way to the express pay-point and took her place in the queue. He stacked his empty basket and waited on the other side of the cash-points, impersonating a bewildered husband waiting for the wife he'd lost sight of. He watched her counting her coins from a small black purse. The transaction seemed to fluster her, as if she might not have enough money to pay for the few things she'd bought. A tin of lentil soup. An individual chicken pie. One solitary tomato. Maybe she did need the avocados – or something else.

5   Some shoplifters used the pay-point: it was like declaring something when you went through customs, in the hope that the real contraband would go unnoticed. An amateur tactic. It was easy to catch someone with a conscience, someone who wanted to be caught.

6   He ambled behind her to the escalator down to Kitchen and Garden. When she came off the escalator, she waited at the bottom, as if not sure where to find what she was looking for. He moved away from her to the saucepans and busied himself opening up a three-tiered vegetable steamer, then he put the lid back on hastily to follow her to the gardening equipment. She moved past the lawn-mowers and the sprinklers until she came to a display of seed packets.

7   It wasn't often you had this kind of intuition about somebody, but as soon as he saw her looking at the seeds, he was certain she was going to steal them. He moved closer to her, picked up a watering can and weighed it in his hand, as if this was somehow a way of testing it, then he saw her dropping packet after packet into the bag. He followed her to the door and outside, then he put his hand on her shoulder. When she turned round he showed her his identity card. Already she was shaking visibly. Her red-veined cheeks had taken on a hectic colour and tears loomed behind her outraged blue eyes . . .

8   "Please," she said, "arrest me. Before I do something worse."

9   He took her back inside and they made the long journey to the top of the store in silence. For the last leg of it he took her through Fabrics – wondering if they might be taken for a couple, a sad old couple shopping together in silence – and up the back staircase so that he wouldn't have to march her through Admin.

10   It was depressing to unlock the door of his cubby-hole, switch the light on and see the table barely big enough to hold his kettle and his tea things, the one upright chair, the barred window looking out on a fire-escape and the wall-mounted telephone. He asked her to take the packets of seeds out of her bag and put them on the table. She did so, and the sight of the packets, with their gaudy coloured photographs of flowers, made her clench her hand into a fist.

11   He told her to take a seat while he called security, but when he turned away from her she let out a thin wail that made him recoil from the phone. She had both her temples between her hands, as if afraid her head might explode. She let out another shrill wail. It ripped out of her like something wild kept prisoner for years. It seemed to make the room shrink around them.

12   She wailed again – a raw outpouring of anger and loss.

13   "Look, you don't seem like a habitual shoplifter . . ."

14   She blurted out that she'd never stolen anything in her life before, but it was hard to make out the words because she was sobbing, and coughing at the same time, her meagre body shuddering as if an invisible man had taken her by the shoulders and was shaking her violently.

15   "I'm sure it was just absent-mindedness. You intended to pay for these." He motioned with a hand to the scattered packets of seeds on the table, but she was having none of it.

16   "No, I stole them. I don't even like gardening." The words came out in spurts between her coughs and sobs but there was no stopping her now that she'd started: "It's overgrown, weeds everywhere. It was him who did it. He was mad about his garden. He spent all his time, morning till night, out in all weathers."

17   Relieved that she was talking rather than wailing, he let her talk. Her husband had been obsessed with his garden. It had been his way of getting away – from her, from everyone and everything. He'd withdrawn from the world into his flowering shrubs and geraniums. She hardly saw him, and when he'd died all there was left of him was his garden. Now the weeds were taking over. When she'd seen the seed packets, with their pictures of dahlias and pansies and rhododendrons . . . It made a kind of sense. Why had she stolen them rather than pay for them? He should have known better than to ask. He got the whole story of her financial hardship now that she was on her own, including the cost of the funeral. It was an expensive business, dying.

[Turn over

18   When she'd finished, she fished a small white handkerchief from her coat pocket to wipe the tears from her eyes. It was the way she did this that reminded him of his mother, the way she had to move her glasses out of the way to get the handkerchief to her eyes.

19   "What are you going to do with me?" she said.

Adapted from the short story "An Invisible Man" by Brian McCabe

[END OF PASSAGE]

FOR OFFICIAL USE

C

Total Mark

0860/406

NATIONAL QUALIFICATIONS 2002

TUESDAY, 7 MAY
2.30 PM – 3.20 PM

ENGLISH
STANDARD GRADE
Credit Level
Reading
Questions

Fill in these boxes and read what is printed below.

Full name of centre

Town

Forename(s)

Surname

Date of birth
Day Month Year

Scottish candidate number

Number of seat

NB Before leaving the examination room you must give this booklet to the invigilator. If you do not, you may lose all the marks for this paper.

SCOTTISH
QUALIFICATIONS
AUTHORITY

MCB 0860/406 6/43270

QUESTIONS

Write your answers in the spaces provided.

Look at Paragraph 1.

1. What **two** things were required of the store detective in order to do his job well?

   (i) _____

   (ii) _____

2. (*a*) Explain what concerns the detective had about:

   (i) kids;

   _____

   _____

   (ii) well-dressed gentlemen.

   _____

   _____

   (*b*) Why do you think **the writer** uses "kids" and "well-dressed gentlemen" as examples?

   _____

   _____

3. Explain why it is appropriate to describe the shoppers as "a plague".

   _____

   _____

Look at Paragraphs 2 to 4.

4. What did the detective do to avoid being noticed in the food hall?

   _____

   _____

Marks

5. Look closely at the final sentence of Paragraph 2.

Identify any **one technique** used by the writer and explain how it helps to create the impression that "The Public was all over the shop".

_____

_____

_____ 2 1 0

6. (*a*) What was the woman doing when the detective first noticed her?

_____ 2 ■ 0

(*b*) **Quote** the expression which best suggests why he followed her to the pay-point.

_____

_____ 2 ■ 0

7. **In your own words** describe what the detective did to avoid being noticed at the pay-point.

_____

_____ 2 1 0

8. In Paragraph 4, how does the writer emphasise that the woman had bought "few things"

(i) by word-choice?

_____

_____ 2 1 0

(ii) by sentence structure?

_____

_____ 2 1 0

[Turn over

PAGE
TOTAL

Look at Paragraphs 5 to 8.

9. (a) The writer compares some shoplifters' use of the pay-point to "declaring something when you went through customs".

Explain fully why this is an appropriate comparison.

_____

_____

_____ 2

(b) Quote an expression which shows that the store detective thought shoplifters were usually unsuccessful when they used the pay-point.

_____

_____ 2

10. "It wasn't often you had this kind of intuition . . ."

How does the rest of Paragraph 7 help to explain the meaning of "intuition"?

_____

_____ 2

11. " 'Please,' she said, 'arrest me. Before I do something worse.' "

Tick (✓) the appropriate box to show which of the following **best** describes your reaction to this statement.

surprised	
intrigued	
not surprised	
sympathetic	

Justify your choice by **close reference to the text**.

_____

_____

_____

_____ 2

Look at Paragraphs 9 and 10.

Marks

12. **In your own words** give **two** pieces of evidence which suggest the detective felt some sympathy towards the woman.

(i) _____

_____ 2 1 0

(ii) _____

_____ 2 1 0

13. The detective found the sight of his cubby-hole "depressing".
Explain how the writer continues this idea in Paragraph 10.

_____

_____ 2 1 0

Look at Paragraphs 11 to 13.

14. Quote a comparison from this section which shows how emotional or upset the woman was, and explain how effective you find it.

_____

_____

_____ 2 1 0

Look at Paragraphs 14 to 16.

15. What further evidence is there in this section that the detective showed some sympathy towards the woman?

_____

_____ 2 ■ 0

[Turn over for Questions 16 to 19 on *Page six*

PAGE
TOTAL

Ma

Look at Paragraphs 17 and 18.

16. Explain clearly why the woman's need for the seed packets "made a kind of sense".

_____

_____

_____   2 1

Think about the passage as a whole.

17. In Paragraph 12 the writer describes the woman's wailing as a "raw outpouring of **anger** and **loss**".

Explain clearly how these emotions relate to her relationship with her husband.

_____

_____

_____   2 1

18. Consider carefully all you have learned about the store detective and the woman.

Supporting your answer by detailed reference to the text, explain whether you think the detective will have the woman charged, or let her go.

_____

_____

_____   2 1

19. The story's title, "An Invisible Man", relates mainly to the store detective.

In what other way does the writer use the idea of an invisible man in the story?

_____

_____

_____   2 1

[END OF QUESTION PAPER]

PAC
TOT

[BLANK PAGE]

G

0860/403

NATIONAL
QUALIFICATIONS
2003

TUESDAY, 6 MAY
1.00 PM – 1.50 PM

ENGLISH
STANDARD GRADE
General Level
Reading
Text

Read carefully the passage overleaf. It will help if you read it twice. When you have done so, answer the questions. Use the spaces provided in the Question/Answer booklet.

SCOTTISH
QUALIFICATIONS
AUTHORITY

We're out for the Count

Catriona Marchant and her children discover that Dracula has a big stake in Romania's tourist industry.

The door creaked open. A draught of cold air blew up from the stairs to the dark crypt and the hairs on our arms stood on end. The faint light from the flickering candle disappeared, there was a muffled scream, a sound of running footsteps and then some raised voices.

2   My three brave boys looked at each other and Douglas, the middle one, ran from the room. The eldest, Matthew, who had been taunting his younger brothers about being scared five minutes earlier, went a bit white and looked like he was going to change his mind about the visit.

3   We were in Dracula's castle — sited on the remote Tihuta mountain pass where the Victorian Gothic novelist Bram Stoker based the home of his fictitious vampire — two days' carriage ride from Bistrita in northern Transylvania.

4   Downstairs was Count Dracula's coffin in a narrow vault, the walls painted with the dramatic scenes of human victims, wolves, skulls, skeletons and the black-cloaked monster himself, red blood dripping from his pointed fangs. So far on our Romanian holiday the only blood-sucking had been from the mosquitoes in Bucharest. Luckily we had decided to send their father down first as a guinea pig to test out how scary this experience was likely to be for our seven-, five- and two-year-olds.

5   After the screams from the crypt, Matthew decided he would opt for a tour with the light on and I agreed. Even so there was a certain nervousness as we went down the stairs. Suddenly, Matthew let out a blood-curdling scream and jumped a foot in the air. "I've just seen a horrible blue hand with long nails, round the side of that door," he screeched.

6   One vampire hand was quite enough for a seven-year-old. Time for a drink and an ice-cream. As we walked up to the main lobby there was "Vampire" red wine for sale, glass vials of red liquid, wooden stakes and probably some garlic stashed under the counter.

7   As these tacky souvenirs revealed, it wasn't the real Dracula's castle but Hotel Castel Dracula, a three-star hotel built in the mountains to service some nearby ski slopes. The architecture (1980s mock castle) reflected the Dracula movies but the setting amid the dramatic scenery of the Tihuta pass is stunning. The "castle" is circled by bats every

night and the surrounding forests have more wi
bears and wolves than anywhere else in Europe.

8   Bram Stoker's story has become mixed up wi
the historical facts as the novelist based his bloo
sucking fictional vampire on the 15th centu
bloodthirsty Prince Vlad Tepes. Vlad was know
fondly as Vlad the Impaler.

9   The tourist board makes the mo
of this confusion between fiction and history, as t
worldwide fascination with Dracula lures many
visitor to the country. The most we
known sights are the birthplace
Vlad Tepes at the beautiful tow
of Sighisoara and Bran Castle, commonly know
as Dracula's Castle.

10   Bran Castle is certainly dramatic, perched
the edge of a rock peak, its ramparts standing o
against the dark mountain backdrop. But as it wa
the former summer royal residence, parts of
inside seem rather cosy and welcoming. Th
ruined castle of Rasnov seems a more suitab
location for a Dracula film, with 360-degree view
of the Carpathian Mountains after a steep walk u
the wooded mountain.

11   Matthew did his best to scare the tourists. H
had been reading his Dracula books and dressed u
in a black cloak, cut out some paper fangs an
jumped round corners and down steps.

12   He gained more smiles and laughs than an
signs of horror — but then it was a warm, sunn
August day. He completed his vampire outfit b
choosing wooden daggers for himself and Dougla
from the busy craft market to protect us from an
blood-sucking monsters that might come our wa
(apart from mosquitoes).

Cloak and dagger: Alistair and Matthew had a scream fooling around near the birthplace of Vlad Tepes, the "original Dracula"

3   Dracula's Kiss was an extremely alcoholic, bright scarlet drink. This fiery concoction must have contained a large quantity of the local plum brandy, known as palinca. I drank this at the birthplace of Vlad Tepes in Sighisoara. His house is now a restaurant which offers themed menus such as Dracula's tomato soup and fairly average food.

4   Not all the themed food given to the tourists on the hunt for Count Dracula is poor. One of the best and most exciting meals of the holiday was at the Count Dracula Club in Bucharest. Once the children got over the fear of the stuffed bears and stags on the walls and dog head skulls hanging from the ceiling, the food was fantastic — thick vegetable soup, polenta with stuffed cabbage leaves. The children drank blood orange juice and feasted on thick stew. Down in the cellar was the coffin, with the waiters dressed like vampires and acting for all they were worth.

5   Away from the crypts was hot summer sunshine: we swam in outdoor swimming pools and visited spas with bubbling warm salt lakes. We felt Romania would be a good place to revisit when the boys were older and could hike and camp in the Carpathian wilderness. The most memorable part of our visit to Romania was staying with a delightful family in Sighisoara who loved the children and treated them with kindness as they helped feed their chickens and cook special apple cake.

16   But if we leave the return visit too long things will have changed dramatically. A DraculaLand theme park is planned to be built by a German or American corporation in medieval Sighisoara next year.

17   Local opinion is divided. On the one hand, there is the desire for tourist money and on the other the realisation that the theme park will change the character of the small town forever. If the cobbled streets are lined with fast food chains offering "stakeburgers" and garlic bread — Dracula will be turning in his grave.

Adapted from an article by
Catriona Marchant

[END OF PASSAGE]

FOR OFFICIAL USE

G

Total
Mark

0860/404

NATIONAL
QUALIFICATIONS
2003

TUESDAY, 6 MAY
1.00 PM – 1.50 PM

ENGLISH
General Level
Reading
Questions

Fill in these boxes and read what is printed below.

Full name of centre

Town

Forename(s)

Surname

Date of birth
Day Month Year

Scottish candidate number

Number of seat

**NB Before leaving the examination room you must give this booklet to the invigilator.
If you do not, you may lose all the marks for this paper.**

SCOTTISH
QUALIFICATIONS
AUTHORITY

©

QUESTIONS

Write your answers in the spaces provided.

Look at Paragraph 1.

1. **In what two ways** does the writer create a frightening atmosphere in the opening sentence?

   (i) _____

   (ii) _____

2. Explain fully what the writer suggests by using the word "flickering" when describing the candle.

   _____

   _____

Look at Paragraph 2.

3. "My three brave boys"

   Explain fully why this expression might be considered to be surprising.

   _____

   _____

4. **Explain in your own words** how Matthew had been treating his brothers.

   _____

Look at Paragraph 3.

5. **Give two pieces of evidence** which suggest that Bram Stoker wrote the novel *Dracula* more than one hundred years ago.

   (i) _____

   (ii) _____

6. Why does the writer use dashes in Paragraph 3?

   _____

Look at Paragraph 4.

Marks

7. "Downstairs was Count Dracula's coffin in a narrow vault, the walls painted with the dramatic scenes"

   In what ways does the writer convey the "dramatic scenes" in the vault?

   _____

   _____

   _____   2 1 0

8. What effect does the writer create by using the expression "So far on our Romanian holiday the only blood-sucking had been from the mosquitoes"?

   _____

   _____   2 ■ 0

9. **In your own words** explain fully why their father was sent down first.

   _____

   _____   2 1 0

Look at Paragraphs 5, 6 and 7.

10. **Write down an expression** which shows that Matthew did not complete the tour.

    _____   2 ■ 0

11. **In your own words** what is the writer's attitude to the various goods for sale in the hotel lobby?

    _____   2 ■ 0

12. **In your own words** what is the writer's opinion of the setting of the Hotel Castel Dracula?

    _____

    _____   2 ■ 0

13. Why does the writer place the word "castle" in inverted commas?

    _____   2 ■ 0

Ma

Look at Paragraphs 8 and 9.

14. What was the real name of the original Dracula?

_____ 2 ■

15. Explain **in your own words** how Romania benefits from "this confusion between fiction and history".

_____

_____ 2 1

Look at Paragraph 10.

16. What contrasting impressions does the writer give of Bran Castle?

_____

_____ 2 1

Look at Paragraphs 11, 12 and 13.

17. "He gained more smiles and laughs than any signs of horror"

Give two reasons why Matthew was an unconvincing vampire.

_____

_____ 2 1

18. What does the expression "fiery concoction" suggest about the Dracula's Kiss drink?

_____

_____ 2 1

Marks

Look at Paragraph 14.

19. (a) **In your own words explain how** the boys felt at the start of their visit to the Count Dracula Club. **Why** did they feel this way?

_____

_____   2 | 1 | 0

(b) **Write down an expression** which clearly shows that the boys changed their attitude to the visit.

_____

_____   2 | ■ | 0

Look at Paragraphs 15, 16 and 17.

20. What kind of holiday in Romania might the writer consider in the future?

_____

_____   2 | 1 | 0

21. (a) How does the writer feel about the changes planned for the tourist industry in Romania?

_____   2 | ■ | 0

(b) Explain **in your own words** how the local people feel about the planned changes.

_____

_____   2 | 1 | 0

(c) "Dracula will be turning in his grave."

Why does the writer finish off the final sentence in this way?

_____

_____   2 | 1 | 0

[Turn over for Question 22 on _Page six_

PAGE
TOTAL

Think about the passage as a whole.

22. "Catriona Marchant and her children discover that Dracula has a big stake in Romania's tourist industry."

Explain fully what is appropriate about this sub-title.

_____

_____

_____   2

[END OF QUESTION PAPER]

2003 Reading | Credit

[BLANK PAGE]

C

0860/405

NATIONAL QUALIFICATIONS 2003	TUESDAY, 6 MAY 2.30 PM – 3.20 PM	ENGLISH STANDARD GRADE Credit Level Reading Text

Read carefully the passage overleaf. It will help if you read it twice. When you have done so, answer the questions. Use the spaces provided in the Question/Answer booklet.

SCOTTISH QUALIFICATIONS AUTHORITY

©

WHY THE I

Scientists have at last dispelled the myth and pieced together the events that led to the extinction of this ridiculous, flightless bird

1   DODO. The very word conjures up an image — fat, stupid, ridiculous. Somehow we feel we know this bird. But one thing we all know is that it's dead. As dead as . . . er . . . the dodo. It's all in the name. It has that sort of childish, sing-song feel to it. Endearing because it sounds so daft. And yet the dodo is more than a cheap laugh: the dodo is an icon. It's a creature of legend, a myth like the Phoenix or the Griffin. But it's a myth that really existed. A living creature so bizarre it didn't need the human imagination to think it up — and an enigma from virtually the first moment human beings laid eyes on it a little more than 500 years ago.

2   Three hundred and fifty years later, Lewis Carroll famously caricatured the bird in *Alice in Wonderland*. He portrayed it as a pompous Victorian gentleman, complete with walking cane. With this, the dodo's journey from "real" to "surreal" was complete.

3   The story begins in Shakespeare's day. In 1598, the crew of the Dutch East Indiaman, The Amsterdam, were navigating round the Cape of Good Hope when a storm blew up and the ship was blown off course. After three weeks adrift, their battered vessel came within sight of a tropical island which they named Mauritius. They were now in the Indian Ocean and the island was a god-send. It meant they could rest and repair their boat — but most importantly it meant the half-starved crew could eat.

4   The fateful encounter now unfolded. The crew quickly came across a large bird, apparently flightless. Then, unable to evade its captors, it was quickly seized by the sailors. It was like nothing they had ever set eyes on.

5   Round in shape with a plume of tail feathers, the bird stood about three feet high, the size of an overstuffed turkey or swan. Its wings were small and useless, its head surrounded by a hood of fine feathers giving it the appearance of a monk's cowl. Yet most distinctive of all was its unfeasible-looking bill. It was huge and bulbous, possessing a businesslike hook at the end.

6   But why did the bird come to be called the dodo? It has been argued that the name reflects the bird's nonsensical appearance. Or that it sounds like the noise the bird may have made. In fact the name dodo didn't stick until other names had been tried — "Kermis" after a Dutch annual fair, then "walghvogel" which means "nauseating fowl". The name "dodo" came when the Dutch finally saw its comical side.

FATEFUL ENCOUNTER: The Dutch cap[t] several of the weird birds

7   Dodomania was born. Soon Dutch artists copying the first drawings of the bird including them in the fantastical "mena[g] paintings that were all the rage. Several birds captured and brought back to Eu One found its way to London, where it displayed for the benefit of paying customer around the time Charles II had been retur[n] the throne of England in 1660, the dodo had forever. What had happened to the dodo? Fi out has not been easy. Following its disappea[r] all anyone had to go on were sketches paintings. All the living specimens that had brought back to Europe were long dead. were no skeletons of the bird in museums. Ra the trail of the dodo began to go cold.

8   Surely this ridiculous bird, fat, flightless vulnerable, had simply been caught and eat extinction? Too weak or stupid to defend itse trusting of humans, the dodo had met its inev end. In a Darwinian world the dodo has down to us as the prime example of how [p] designed and hapless creatures just won't s[t] the race. Sad but inevitable sums up the exti[r] of the dodo. Until now. According to ornitho Julian Hume, the fat, comical appearance bird is grossly exaggerated. Julian has travell Mauritius to investigate what the bird was like and how it lived. It is here that the onl complete skeletons of the bird exist which proved just how misrepresented the dodo has "Now we have the skeleton of the dodo, we c[a] so much more about the bird and how it may appeared in life," says Julian. "It had a sinuous neck, quite an upright stance, probably stood about two and a half feet tall. is very different from the picture that's come to us from those early drawings."

⌐ IS DEAD

IGHT OF FANCY: New research has shown at the dodo was not the fat, squat bird drawn ʳ 18th century artists, rather a lean, upright ʳeature with a powerful hooked bill

The dodo wasn't a fat, squat creature; it was ɑn and upright. Indeed, the earliest images, ɑwn from life, show a scrawny bird, its hooked ʟl making its appearance quite aggressive. The ʈer you go, the fatter and sillier it becomes. ʈhere are many other mysteries to solve. Why was ⌐ flightless? Why did it live on Mauritius ʌd nowhere else? How did it get there? Finding ɯt takes us right back to the 17th century.

When the London dodo died, the animal was ʌffed and sold to the Ashmolean Museum in ⌐xford. Taxidermy not being what it is today, over ⌐e next few decades the dodo slowly rotted until it ⌐s thrown out in 1755. All, that is, except the ⌐oth-eaten head and one leg.

Today these remnants are the only surviving ⌐do skin tissue in existence.

For more than a century scientists had assumed ⌐at the dodo's ancestors must have reached ⌐auritius from Africa — because this is the nearest ⌐ntinental land mass. In fact, Dr Shapiro has ⌐oved the dodo was south-east Asian. Its closest ⌐cestor spent millions of years island-hopping ⌐om somewhere in the region of Burma or ⌐donesia until it finally arrived on Mauritius. ⌐here it stayed and, unthreatened by predators, ⌐ve up the ability to fly, massively increased in ⌐ze and became the creature that the Dutch finally ⌐n into in 1598.

13 Julian Hume believes the bird rooted at ground level, foraging fruits from palm trees and using its tough bill to break open and eat snail shells. It built its nest on the forest floor into which it had laid a single egg, possibly only every other year.

14 The dodo was master of its domain, superbly and uniquely adapted to its particular environment. Yet within 70 years of its discovery by man, it was extinct.

15 Dutch archaeologist Pieter Floore has spent several seasons excavating the rubbish dumps left by the Mauritanian Dutch colonists at Fort Hendrink, their main base. If they hunted the dodo to extinction, Floore reckoned he would be able to find evidence in the form of dodo bones among the household rubbish the Dutch threw out.

16 Yet despite several years of digging, he has not found a single dodo bone. In fact, there is no evidence whatsoever that the Dutch ever hunted and ate the dodo on any scale that would lead to its extinction.

17 Combining evidence from the skeleton and other written accounts, Julian Hume has also demonstrated that the dodo was not only quite hard to catch, but was also terrible to eat. Being flightless, it had no breast muscles and hence no breast meat. Its fat bottom was meaty but so greasy that accounts reveal that it "cloyed and nauseated the stomach" — hence the original name "walghvogel" or "nauseating fowl".

18 Yet still it perished. Just why has been revealed by archaeologist Pieter Floore. While he has never found a single dodo bone, he has uncovered tens of thousands of bones belonging to animals that the Dutch introduced to the island. Most visible are the bones of pigs, and these provide the vital clue.

19 Pigs, like dodos, are ground-rooting animals. They are easy to farm — simply release them into the forest and they will take care of themselves. As they did so they proved fatal to the dodo, disturbing ancient mating and nesting behaviour, eating the dodo's eggs, and voraciously competing for food. In Mauritius's unique island habitat, perfectly balanced for more than 10 million years, something as apparently benign as the introduction of the pig proved fatal for the dodo.

20 When a German sailor was shipwrecked on Mauritius in 1662, he walked the length and breadth of the island but saw no dodos except a few on an islet off-shore. This was the last dodo colony seen by man.

21 By 1670 the last dodo was dead and the bird had passed from reality into myth. Only now have we found the real reason why.

Adapted from an article by *Alex West*

[END OF PASSAGE]

[BLANK PAGE]

FOR OFFICIAL USE

C

Total Mark

0860/406

NATIONAL
QUALIFICATIONS
2003

TUESDAY, 6 MAY
2.30 PM – 3.20 PM

ENGLISH
STANDARD GRADE
Credit Level
Reading
Questions

Fill in these boxes and read what is printed below.

Full name of centre

Town

Forename(s)

Surname

Date of birth
Day   Month   Year   Scottish candidate number   Number of seat

NB Before leaving the examination room you must give this booklet to the invigilator. If you do not, you may lose all the marks for this paper.

SCOTTISH
QUALIFICATIONS
AUTHORITY

SAB 0860/406 6/44470

©

QUESTIONS

Write your answers in the spaces provided.

Look at Paragraphs 1 and 2.

1. Explain why the writer opens the passage with the single word "DODO".

   _____   **2 1**

2. **According to the writer** why is the name of the dodo both familiar and memorable?

   _____

   _____   **2 1**

3. Explain fully what is unusual about the expression "But it's a myth that really existed".

   _____

   _____

   _____   **2 1**

4. Which **two** words does the writer use to emphasise the strangeness of the dodo?   **2 1**

   (i) _____

   (ii) _____

5. "Lewis Carroll famously caricatured the bird"

   Explain fully how the rest of Paragraph 2 develops this idea.

   _____

   _____

   _____   **2 1**

Marks

Look at Paragraphs 3 to 6.

6. What does the writer's use of the expression "fateful encounter" tell you about the meeting?

_____

_____ 2 ■ 0

7. "It was like nothing they had ever set eyes on."

What is the function of this sentence?

_____ 2 ■ 0

8. In your own words, what does the writer's use of the expression "unfeasible-looking" tell you about the dodo's bill?

_____

_____ 2 1 0

9. Explain the writer's use of a question at the beginning of Paragraph 6.

_____

_____ 2 1 0

Look at Paragraph 7.

10. What examples of Dodomania does the writer give? Answer in your own words.

_____

_____

_____ 2 1 0

[Turn over

PAGE
TOTAL

Ma

11. "Rapidly, the trail of the dodo began to go cold."

Why do you think the writer chooses to use this expression?

_____

_____ 2

Look at Paragraphs 8 to 11.

12. Explain **in your own words** why the dodo is a good example of the theories of the "Darwinian world".

_____

_____ 2

13. Which **one word** in Paragraph 8 sums up the writer's sympathetic attitude to the dodo?

_____ 2

14. Give details of **two** obvious contrasts between the imagined appearance and the real appearance of the dodo. 2

(i) _____

(ii) _____

15. Why does the writer use a series of questions in Paragraph 9?

_____

_____ 2

16. Explain how the context helps you to understand the meaning of "taxidermy" in Paragraph 10.

_____

_____ 2

PA
TO

Marks

Look at Paragraph 12.

17. Explain fully, **in your own words**, why the scientists "assumed" that the dodo reached Mauritius from Africa.

_____

_____ 2 1 0

18. Explain fully why you think the writer chooses to use the expression "island-hopping".

_____

_____

_____ 2 1 0

Look at Paragraphs 13 to 18.

19. Quote **two** expressions which suggest that Julian Hume's knowledge of the dodo is theoretical. 2 1 0

(i) _____

(ii) _____

20. What **two** pieces of evidence helped prove that the Dutch did not hunt the dodo to extinction? 2 1 0

(i) _____

(ii) _____

[Turn over for Questions 21 to 25 on *Page six*

PAGE
TOTAL

Look at Paragraphs 19 to 21.

21. **In your own words**, explain fully why the introduction of pigs proved "fatal" for the dodo.

_____

_____

_____ 2

22. What does the writer's use of the expression "apparently benign" tell you about the introduction of the pigs?

_____

_____ 2

23. Why does the writer give the dates in the final two paragraphs?

_____

_____ 2

Think about the passage as a whole.

24. The purpose of the article is to provide scientific information in a popular format. By close reference to the text, identify and comment on any technique which the writer uses to add weight to the information.

_____

_____

_____

_____ 2

25. What **two key questions** are answered as a result of the information in the passage?

_____

_____

_____ 2

[END OF QUESTION PAPER]

[BLANK PAGE]

G

0860/403

NATIONAL QUALIFICATIONS 2004	WEDNESDAY, 5 MAY 1.00 PM – 1.50 PM	**ENGLISH STANDARD GRADE** General Level Reading Text

Read carefully the passage overleaf. It will help if you read it twice. When you have done so, answer the questions. Use the spaces provided in the Question/Answer booklet.

SCOTTISH QUALIFICATIONS AUTHORITY

Pucker Way to Kiss a Hummingbird

Mark Carwardine puts on lipstick in Arizona for a wild encounter.

SUMMER SPECTACLE:
Thousands of hummingbirds arrive in Arizona every y

1   There's a rather embarrassing tradition in wildlife circles in certain parts of Arizona. Visiting naturalists are encouraged to try to "kiss" a wild hummingbird.

2   This is more of a challenge for men than it is for women – mainly because it involves wearing lots of red lipstick. A dress and high heels are optional, but the redder and thicker the lipstick the better. Hummingbirds drink nectar from flowers that are often bright red and have learned to associate this particular colour with food. They mistake your mouth for one of their favourite plants – at least, that's the theory.

3   Which is how I found myself high in the mountains of South-East Arizona, with puckered lips pointing sky-ward and a crowd of bemused onlookers egging me on.

4   My home for a couple of days was Beatty's Guest Ranch near the Mexico border. Run by Tom and Edith Beatty, the ranch is nearly 6,000ft above sea level, nestling between two enormous peaks, with spectacular views down the valley to the desert below.

5   According to the South-Eastern Arizona Bird Observatory, it is the hottest hummingbird-watching spot in the state. Thousands of "hummers" arrive in April and May and stay until early October. No fewer than 15 different species are found here on a regular basis.

6   Dozens of special hummingbird feeders, looking like upside-down jam jars, are dotted around the ranch. Hanging from trees, bushes, fences and buildings they are full of a simple magic potion (four parts water, one part white sugar) similar to the nectar of hummingbird flowers. Tom and Edith keep the feeders topped up, getting through a mind-boggling 550 2lb bags of sugar in a typical year.

7   There were two feeders outside my bedroom window in the turn-of-th century self-catering cabin on the for edge (not a good place to stay if you've se *Friday The 13th* or *The Blair Witch Proje* but idyllic in every other sense).

8   I will never forget pulling back the curtai on the first morning. There we hummingbirds everywhere, whizzi backwards and forwards past the wind like demented bees. Sometimes th paused in front of the sugar-water to fee either perching or hovering with t immaculate precision of experienc helicopter pilots.

9   Apparently, it's possible to see as many ten species at the ranch in just half an ho But even when they stayed still for mc than a few moments I had no idea whi was which. As they moved around, th colours changed in relation to the angle the sun. Bird identification is hard enou at the best of times, but this was ridiculou

10   Take a male hummingbird, for examp When you look at it face-to-face its throat a fiery scarlet red. But as it turns away t colour shifts – first to orange, then yello then blackish-brown and then green. T identifying that in a hurry, before it tur

into a blur and helicopters away.

1 I think there were Anna's hummingbirds, black-chinned, broad billed, blue-throated, magnificent, red and violet-crowned that morning, but I'm not entirely sure. Later, I asked other bird-watchers about similar-looking hummers around "their" feeding station, but they weren't sure either. I left them bickering over the difference between the sapphire blue throat of a broad-bill and the cobalt blue throat of a blue-throat.

2 The biological advantage of changing colour is that the birds can control the way they look. If a male wants to impress a female he shows his best side, but if he wants to hide from a predator he merely turns away and almost disappears among the greenery.

3 According to Sheri Williamson, hummingbird expert and co-founder of the South-Eastern Arizona Bird Observatory, you can tell them apart by the sound of their wings. Broad-tailed hummingbirds, for example, have a metallic trill to their wingbeats, while male black-chinned hummingbirds make a dull, flat whine.

4 Sheri took me to see a hummingbird in the hand. There's a ringing station, or banding station as they call it in the States, at nearby Sierra Vista. It's open to the public and every weekend the observatory staff rig up a mist-net trap with a tasty-looking sugar-water feeder in the middle. Whenever a hummingbird dares an investigatory hover, a burly member of the observatory team rushes forward, waving his arms around, and ushers the unfortunate bird inside.

5 We caught lots of hummingbirds that day. One was a female black-chinned that squealed when she was caught. It was hard to tell whether this was out of fear or anger ("How could I, so fleet of wing, be caught by this enormous fool?"). We found her abdomen distended with an enormous egg, which Sheri guessed would be laid before nightfall.

6 For a brief moment, I actually held the delicate bundle of feathers in my hand, and

was so nervous about squeezing too hard that she escaped. After hovering above us for a moment, she made a bee-line for the bushes.

17 Hovering hummingbirds draw crowds of naturalists from all over the world to South-East Arizona, but hovering does have one major drawback. Pound for pound, beating your wings 70 times per second uses more energy than any other activity in the animal kingdom. Living life in the fast lane means hummingbirds need a continuous supply of fuel.

18 A typical hummingbird eats around half its own weight in energy-rich nectar every day. To do that it has to keep others away from its favourite foodplants. I spent many hours watching them battle it out at feeding stations. Far from being all sweetness and light, they are little fighter pilots. If they were the size of ravens it wouldn't be safe to walk in the woods.

19 Before I left, there was one thing I had to do. Dutifully, I put on bright red lipstick, took a mouthful of sugar-water, sat back, puckered my lips . . . and waited. Within 30 seconds two hummingbirds came to investigate. Others soon followed.

20 I sat there for an eternity not daring to move. No hummingbird actually drank sugar-water from my mouth (who can blame them?), but several did hover so close I could feel their wingbeats against my cheeks.

21 Strangely, the encounter was every bit as impressive as rubbing shoulders with mountain gorillas in the wilds of Africa or performing slow-motion underwater ballets with dolphins in the Bahamas.

22 Even better, my biggest worry came to nothing – the red lipstick wiped off.

(Adapted from an article by Mark Carwardine)

[END OF PASSAGE]

[BLANK PAGE]

G

Total
Mark

0860/404

NATIONAL
QUALIFICATIONS
2004

WEDNESDAY, 5 MAY
1.00 PM – 1.50 PM

ENGLISH
STANDARD GRADE
General Level
Reading
Questions

Fill in these boxes and read what is printed below.

Full name of centre

Town

Forename(s)

Surname

Date of birth
Day Month Year

Scottish candidate number

Number of seat

**NB Before leaving the examination room you must give this booklet to the invigilator.
If you do not, you may lose all the marks for this paper.**

SCOTTISH
QUALIFICATIONS
AUTHORITY

QUESTIONS

Write your answers in the spaces provided.

Look at Paragraphs 1 and 2.

1. **Write down a word** from Paragraph 1 that suggests naturalists might be reluctant to kiss a hummingbird.

    _____   2

2. Why are the hummingbirds attracted to someone wearing bright red lipstick?

    _____

    _____   2

3. Why do you think the writer uses the word "theory" in Paragraph 2?

    _____   2

Look at Paragraphs 3 and 4.

4. Where **exactly** did the writer first meet the hummingbirds?

    _____

    _____   2

Look at Paragraphs 5 and 6.

5. Thousands of "hummers" (Paragraph 5)

    Why has the writer put the word "hummers" in inverted commas?

    _____

    _____   2

Marks

6. "Hanging from trees, bushes, fences and buildings they are full of a simple magic potion . . . flowers." (Paragraph 6)

   Identify and comment on the effect of **two features** of the structure of this sentence.

   (i) _____

   _____   2 1 0

   (ii) _____

   _____   2 1 0

7. **Write down an expression** from Paragraph 6 which tells you that the writer is surprised by the amount of sugar used.

   _____   2 ■ 0

Look at Paragraphs 7 and 8.

8. What do the expressions "whizzing" and "like demented bees" tell you about the movement of the hummingbirds?

   _____

   _____   2 1 0

9. **Write down an expression** which shows that the writer admires the flying skills of the hummingbird.

   _____   2 ■ 0

Look at Paragraphs 9 and 10.

10. **In your own words** write down **two** reasons why the writer found bird identification "ridiculous".   2 1 0

    (i) _____

    (ii) _____

PAGE TOTAL

Ma~

Look at Paragraphs 11 and 12.

11. What does the writer's use of the word "bickering" tell you about his attitude to the bird watchers?

_____ 2

12. **In your own words** give **two** reasons why hummingbirds change their colour. 2 1

    (i) _____

    (ii) _____

Look at Paragraphs 13 to 15.

13. How does Sheri Williamson tell the difference between hummingbirds?

_____

_____ 2 1

14. Comment on the writer's use of the expression "hummingbird in the hand".

_____

_____ 2 1

15. "Whenever a hummingbird dares an investigatory hover, a burly member of the observatory team rushes forward, waving his arms around" (Paragraph 14)

How does this description create effective contrasts?

    (i) _____ 2

    (ii) _____ 2

Look at Paragraph 16.

16. What does the expression "I actually held" tell you about how the writer felt when he held the hummingbird?

_____

_____ 2

PA(
TO1

Marks

Look at Paragraphs 17 and 18.

17. "Living life in the fast lane means hummingbirds need a continuous supply of fuel."
(Paragraph 17)

Explain the effectiveness of this image.

_____

_____

_____ 2 1 0

18. **In your own words**, what **two** new impressions does the writer give of the hummingbird in Paragraph 18?

_____

_____ 2 1 0

Look at Paragraphs 19 to 22.

19. "Dutifully, I put on bright red lipstick . . . puckered my lips . . . and waited."
(Paragraph 19)

Identify and comment on any **one feature** of structure **or** punctuation in this sentence.

_____

_____

_____ 2 1 0

20. **Write down an expression** from Paragraph 20 which tells us the writer felt he waited for a long time.

_____ 2 ■ 0

21. **In your own words** what does the writer's use of the word "Strangely" tell you about his reaction to the encounter with the hummingbirds?

_____

_____ 2 ■ 0

[Turn over for Questions 22 and 23 on *Page six*

PAGE TOTAL

Mark

Think about the passage as a whole.

22. From the passage **write down an example** of the writer's use of humour.

    Explain why it is effective.

    _____

    _____

    _____   2   1

23. Overall how do you think the writer feels about his experience with the humming-birds?

    Support your answer by referring to the passage.

    _____

    _____

    _____   2   1

[END OF QUESTION PAPER]

[BLANK PAGE]

C

0860/405

NATIONAL
QUALIFICATIONS
2004

WEDNESDAY, 5 MAY
2.30 PM – 3.20 PM

ENGLISH
STANDARD GRADE
Credit Level
Reading
Text

Read carefully the passage overleaf. It will help if you read it twice. When you have done so, answer the questions. Use the spaces provided in the Question/Answer booklet.

SCOTTISH
QUALIFICATIONS
AUTHORITY

©

The following extract is taken from a novel set on a Greek island during the Second World War.

1   When Pelagia entered the kitchen she stopped singing abruptly, and was seized with consternation. There was a stranger seated at the kitchen table, a most horrible and wild stranger who looked worse than the brigands of childhood tales. The man was quite motionless except for the rhythmic fluttering and trembling of his hands. His head was utterly concealed beneath a cascade of matted hair that seemed to have no form nor colour. In places it stuck out in twisted corkscrews, and in others it lay in congealed pads like felt; it was the hair of a hermit demented by solitude. Beneath it Pelagia could see nothing but an enormous and disorderly beard surmounted by two tiny bright eyes that would not look at her. There was a nose in there, stripped of its skin, reddened and flaked, and glimpses of darkened, streaked and grimy flesh.

2   The stranger wore the unidentifiable and ragged remains of a shirt and trousers, and a kind of overcoat cut out of animal skins that had been tacked together with thongs of sinew. Pelagia saw, beneath the table, that in place of shoes his feet were bound with bandages that were both caked with old, congealed blood, and the bright stains of fresh. He was breathing heavily, and the smell was inconceivably foul; it was the reek of rotting flesh, of festering wounds, of ancient perspiration, and of fear. She looked at the hands that were clasped together in the effort to prevent their quivering, and was overcome both with fright and pity.   What was she to do?

3   "My father's out," she said. "He should be back tomorrow."

4   "Ice," said the stranger, as though he had not heard her, "I'll never be warm again." His voice cracked and she realised that his shoulders were heaving. "Oh, the ice," he repeated. He held his hands before his face. He wrapped his fingers together, and his whole body seemed to be fighting to suppress a succession of spasms.

5   "You can come back tomorrow," said Pelagia, appalled by this gibbering apparition, and completely at a loss.

6   "No crampons, you see. The snow is whipped away by the wind, and the ice is in ridges, sharper than knives, and when you fall you are cut. Look at my hands." He held them up to her, palm outwards in the gesture that would normally be an insult, and she saw the horrendous cross-tracking of hard white scars that had obliterated every natural line, scored away the pads and calluses, and left seeping cracks across the joints. There were no nails and no trace of cuticles.

7   "And the ice screams. It shrieks. And voices call to you out of it. And you look into it and you see people. They beckon and wave, and they mock, and you shoot into the ice but they don't shut up, and then the ice squeaks. It squeaks all night, all night."

8   "Look, you can't stay," said Pelagia.

9   Her perplexity was growing into an acute anxiety as she wondered what on earth she was supposed to do on her own with a mad vagrant ranting in her kitchen. She thought of leaving him there and running out to fetch help; but was paralysed by the thought of what he might do or steal in her absence. "Please leave," she pleaded. "My father will be back tomorrow, and he can . . . see to your feet."

10   The man responded to her for the first time, "I can't walk. No boots."

11   Psipsina entered the room and sniffed the air, her whiskers twitching as she sampled the strong and unfamiliar smells. She ran across the floor in her fluid

manner, and leapt up onto the table. She approached the neolithic man and burrowed in the remains of a pocket, emerging triumphantly with a small cube of white cheese that she demolished with evident satisfaction. She returned to the pocket and found only a broken cigarette, which she discarded.

12   The man smiled, revealing good teeth but bleeding gums, and he petted the animal about the head. "Ah, at least Psipsina remembers me," he said, and silent tears began to follow each other down his cheeks and into his beard. "She still smells sweet."

13   Pelagia was astounded. Psipsina was afraid of strangers, and how did this ghastly ruin know her name? Who could have told him? She wiped her hands on her apron for the lack of any sense of what to think or do, and said, "Mandras?"

14   The man turned his face towards her and said, "Don't touch me, Pelagia. I've got lice. I didn't know what to do, and I came here first. All the time I knew I had to get here first, that's all, and I'm tired. Do you have any coffee?"

15   Pelagia's mind became void, decentred by a babble of emotions. She felt despair, unbearable excitement, guilt, pity, revulsion. Her heart jumped in her chest and her hands fell to her side. Perhaps more than anything else, she felt helpless. It seemed inconceivable that this desolate ghost concealed the soul and body of the man she had loved and desired and missed so much, and then finally dismissed. "You never wrote to me," she said, coming up with the first thing that entered her head, the accusation that had rankled in her mind from the moment of his departure, the accusation that had grown into an angry, resentful monster.

16   Mandras looked up wearily, and said, as though it were he that pitied her, "I can't write."

17   For a reason that she did not understand, Pelagia was more repelled by this admission than by his filth. Had she betrothed herself to an illiterate, without even knowing it? For the sake of something to say she asked, "Couldn't someone else have written for you? I thought you were dead. I thought you . . . couldn't love me."

Adapted from *Captain Corelli's Mandolin* by Louis de Bernières

[END OF PASSAGE]

[BLANK PAGE]

FOR OFFICIAL USE

C

Total
Mark

0860/406

NATIONAL
QUALIFICATIONS
2004

WEDNESDAY, 5 MAY
2.30 PM – 3.20 PM

ENGLISH
STANDARD GRADE
Credit Level
Reading
Questions

Fill in these boxes and read what is printed below.

Full name of centre

Town

Forename(s)

Surname

Date of birth
Day Month Year   Scottish candidate number   Number of seat

NB Before leaving the examination room you must give this booklet to the invigilator. If you do not, you may lose all the marks for this paper.

SCOTTISH
QUALIFICATIONS
AUTHORITY

SAB 0860/406 6/43820

Ma

QUESTIONS

Write your answers in the spaces provided.

Look at Paragraph 1.

1. Quote **two** words used by the writer to convey the suddenness of Pelagia's reactions as she entered the kitchen.

   (i) _____

   (ii) _____

   | 2 | 1 |

2. Quote the expression which sums up Pelagia's impression of the stranger.

   _____

   | 2 |

3. **In your own words** what contrasting image does the writer give of the movements of the man?

   _____

   | 2 | 1 |

4. What **two** ideas are suggested by the expression "a hermit demented by solitude"?

   | 2 | 1 |

   (i) _____

   (ii) _____

5. Explain fully why it was difficult for Pelagia to get a clear view of the stranger's face.

   _____

   _____

   | 2 | 1 |

Look at Paragraph 2.

6. "congealed blood, and the bright stains of fresh."

   What does this description tell you about the wounds to the man's feet?

   _____

   | 2 | 1 |

PA
TO'

Marks

7. "it was the reek of rotting flesh . . . fear."

Explain fully how the writer emphasises the smell from the stranger

  (i) through sentence structure.

_____

_____   **2** | **1** | **0**

  (ii) through word choice.

_____

_____   **2** | **1** | **0**

8. (*a*) **In your own words** what **two** conflicting emotions did Pelagia feel when she looked at the man?

_____   **2** | **1** | **0**

  (*b*) Explain how the writer conveys Pelagia's dilemma.

_____   **2** | ■ | **0**

Look at Paragraphs 3 to 5.

9. "My father's out," she said. "He should be back tomorrow."

What does Pelagia hope to achieve by making this statement?

_____   **2** | ■ | **0**

10. Why is "gibbering" (Paragraph 5) an appropriate word to describe the stranger at this point?

_____

_____   **2** | **1** | **0**

[Turn over

PAGE
TOTAL

Ma

Look at Paragraphs 6 and 7.

11. What **two** features of the ice disturbed the man most?   2

    (i) _____

    (ii) _____

12. **Identify** any **two techniques** used by the writer in Paragraph 7 which help to
    convey the man's sense of panic and distress.   2

    (i) _____

    (ii) _____

Look at Paragraphs 8 to 10.

13. What are the options that Pelagia is considering in Paragraph 9?

    _____

    _____   2

Look at Paragraphs 11 and 12.

14. Quote **two** words from Paragraph 11 which suggest that Psipsina was unhappy with
    her second visit to the man's pocket.   2

    (i) _____

    (ii) _____

15. "Ah, at least Psipsina remembers me," (Paragraph 12)

    What does this imply about the man's feelings towards Pelagia?

    _____   2

Marks

Look at Paragraphs 13 and 14.

16. "Pelagia was astounded."

    How does the sentence structure in the rest of this paragraph develop Pelagia's sense of astonishment?

    _____

    _____ 2 1 0

17. "The man turned his face towards her and said, 'Don't touch me, Pelagia.'"

    Why might this statement by Mandras be considered ironic?

    _____

    _____ 2 1 0

Look at Paragraphs 15 to 17.

18. Tick (✓) the appropriate box to show which of the following best describes the relationship between Mandras and Pelagia.

    Brother ☐   Father ☐

    Husband ☐   Fiancé ☐

    Justify your answer with close reference to the text.

    _____

    _____ 2 1 0

19. **Identify one way** in which the writer conveys the intensity of Pelagia's feelings about the fact that Mandras had not written.

    _____

    _____ 2 ■ 0

[Turn over for Questions 20 to 22 on *Page six*

PAGE
TOTAL

Mark.

20. **In your own words** explain fully how Pelagia felt when Mandras confessed he could not write.

_____

_____ 2 1

Think about the passage as a whole.

21. How does each of the characters change in the course of the passage? **(Clear change must be indicated.)**

Pelagia _____

_____

_____ 2 1

Mandras _____

_____

_____ 2 1

22. For whom do you feel more sympathy – Pelagia or Mandras?

Justify your choice by close reference to the passage.

_____

_____

_____ 2 1

[END OF QUESTION PAPER]

PAC
TOT

[BLANK PAGE]

G

0860/403

NATIONAL
QUALIFICATIONS
2005

WEDNESDAY, 4 MAY
1.00 PM – 1.50 PM

ENGLISH
STANDARD GRADE
General Level
Reading
Text

Read carefully the passage overleaf. It will help if you read it twice. When you have done so, answer the questions. Use the spaces provided in the Question/Answer booklet.

SCOTTISH
QUALIFICATIONS
AUTHORITY

©

Dazzled by the Stars

Our love affair with fame may be bad for our health, according to new research. **John Harlow** reports on "celebrity worship syndrome".

1 Under her bed Katherine Hicks keeps six years of yellowing newspaper clippings about the former pop band Boyzone, and 70 videos of their performances. There might have been more if her attention had not moved on to Westlife, another pop sensation.

2 In one year she has spent £3,000 to watch Westlife perform 17 times, and is such a regular concert fan that she believes the band now recognise her as an acquaintance, if not a friend.

3 She has fixed her sights on a new star: David Sneddon, first winner of the television show Fame Academy. She cornered Sneddon at two television appearances, though it is early days in her "acquaintance" with him. Yet she felt forced to defend him indignantly against a TV presenter who, she thought, had not shown Sneddon sufficient respect.

4 Hicks is no deluded young teen: she is a 28-year-old electrical engineer. But she freely admits to an "addiction" to the latest musical sensations. "I have an obsessive nature. Anything I do is full-on, but it has never caused me problems," she said last week. "I don't do anything I cannot afford, and I don't ring in sick at work to get time off."

5 She is no stalker or obsessive; she is just "fascinated by the real personas of these people". Though she likens her behaviour to an "addiction rather than an illness", she sees nothing odd in it.

6 "Other people think I am ill or sad," she said, "but I am not missing out on anything."

7 Psychologists, who are taking an increasing interest in the effects of celebrity culture, might disagree. As Anglo-American research published last week reveals, our relationship with celebrities is more complicated than we realise. The strength of our interest in celebrities, say academics, may affect our mood.

8 Lynn McCutcheon, of DeVry University in Florida, John Maltby, of Leicester University, and two colleagues will publish a book next year exposing the psychological needs and drives behind celebrity worship.

9 But initial results of research they have conducted show that about a third of people suffer from what the researchers call "celebrity worship syndrome" and it affects their mental wellbeing.

10 It raises a troubling question: in the era of "industrialised fame", is hero worship bad for you?

11 Perhaps we should blame the start of it on Alexander the Great who, more than 2,000 years ago, exploited to the full the idea of the beautiful "god-king".

12 But if celebrity has been a cultural phenomenon for centuries, why should it have become a problem now? McCutcheon and Maltby believe the scale of it has made a huge jump in recent years. The average westerner is now exposed to hundreds of star images every day through advertising, broadcasting, fashion, the internet and innumerable other forms.

13 Though sales of some celebrity magazines are slipping, figures show that new publications are thriving. In America the thirst for star images is so strong that one photographer was recently paid £70,000 for a single picture.

14 David Beckham is now so famous that one paper set out on a humorous quest to find someone who did not know who he was: they finally tracked down an innocent in the Saharan city of Timbuktu.

15 The rapid growth of fan-based internet sites spreads gossip, the lifeblood of celebrity, at lightning speed. There are

more than 100,000 sites dedicated to Madonna alone.

16 Such a speedy development has prompted the academics to create the celebrity attitude scale. Using a series of questions designed to gauge personality and the level of interest in celebrities, they surveyed 700 people.

17 Most were just casually interested in stars. But one in five people displayed a determined interest. They even rearrange their social lives, for example, to follow their chosen celebrity.

18 Some 10% of people displayed such "intense-personal" attitudes towards celebrities that they showed signs of addiction.

19 It can lead to extreme actions. On both sides of the Atlantic, some fans have resorted to plastic surgery to look more like their heroes. A Scottish actor had himself turned into a Pierce Brosnan lookalike and admits he now often walks and talks like 007.

20 Dr Nicholas Chugay, a Beverly Hills surgeon, has turned various Californians into Elvis Presley or Cher. "I have had to turn some people away because I do not feel it would be good for them to let such worship take over their lives," said Chugay.

21 BUT it may not be all that bad. Indeed, other academics argue that the likes of Beckham and Madonna are even good for you. They say that celebrity culture is based on sound reasons: by watching and imitating our so-called betters, whether it be in clothes or habits, we learn to flourish in human society.

22 Francisco Gil-White, of Pennsylvania University, argues we need celebrities to show us the road to success. He says they provide the educational and entertaining fables once sought in fairy tales.

23 "It makes sense to copy winners, because whoever is getting more of what everybody wants, and in this society this includes media attention, is probably using successful methods to get it."

24 But though some role models, such as Gareth Gates, the singer, and Tiger Woods, the golfer, can maintain they are blazing a trail for others to follow, can less worthy idols cause damage? Nancy Salzburg, who is researching charisma at San Diego University, said bad idols can cause trouble for their followers.

25 Choose well and there are benefits in celebrity, says Maltby. "It may help people to develop a relationship with and understand the world. If you admire someone like David Beckham, for example, and follow his dietary regime and the way he plays football, there can be a positive outcome in doing that."

26 Mark Griffiths, a professor of psychology at Nottingham Trent University, agrees.

27 "It was quite clear that for fans their idols formed a healthy part of their life," he said. "It was a way of raising their self-esteem.

28 What has happened is that people are not so religious and they don't look up to political and religious leaders any more. They have been replaced by the David Beckhams and the pop stars and film stars. That's who you see on the walls of teenagers' rooms because these are the people they look up to and admire."

Adapted from an article by
John Harlow

[*END OF PASSAGE*]

[BLANK PAGE]

FOR OFFICIAL USE

G

Total
Mark

0860/404

NATIONAL
QUALIFICATIONS
2005

WEDNESDAY, 4 MAY
1.00 PM – 1.50 PM

ENGLISH
STANDARD GRADE
General Level
Reading
Questions

Fill in these boxes and read what is printed below.

Full name of centre

Town

Forename(s)

Surname

Date of birth
Day Month Year

Scottish candidate number

Number of seat

**NB Before leaving the examination room you must give this booklet to the invigilator.
If you do not, you may lose all the marks for this paper.**

SCOTTISH
QUALIFICATIONS
AUTHORITY

©

QUESTIONS

Write your answers in the spaces provided.

Look at Paragraphs 1 and 2.

1. What evidence is there to suggest that Katherine Hicks was a keen fan of Boyzone?

_____

_____

2. **Write down three key facts** which clearly show that Katherine Hicks is now a keen Westlife fan.

   (i) _____

   (ii) _____

   (iii) _____

Look at Paragraph 3.

3. Why do you think the writer uses the expression "fixed her sights"?

_____

_____

4. "early days in her "acquaintance" with him"

   Why has the writer put the word "acquaintance" in inverted commas?

_____

_____

5. What do the words "forced" and "indignantly" in Paragraph 3 tell you about Katherine's reactions to the TV presenter's treatment of David Sneddon?

_____

Marks

Look at Paragraphs 4 to 6.

6. "Hicks is no deluded young teen: she is a 28-year-old electrical engineer." (Paragraph 4)

   What does this statement tell you about the writer's attitude towards Katherine's behaviour?

   _____

   2 ■ 0

7. (a) Which of the following best describes Katherine's attitude towards her "addiction"?

   Tick (✓) the appropriate box.

   Concerned ☐

   Guilty ☐

   Relaxed ☐

   2 ■ 0

   (b) **Quote an expression** to support your answer.

   _____

   2 ■ 0

Look at Paragraphs 7 to 10.

8. **Give three reasons** why psychologists are showing an increasing interest in "celebrity culture".

   (i) _____

   (ii) _____

   (iii) _____

   2 1 0

9. Explain why the writer ends Paragraph 10 with a question.

   _____

   2 ■ 0

Marks

Look at Paragraphs 11 to 14.

10. Who does the writer suggest is to blame for the start of hero worship?

_____

2

11. **Quote an expression** which shows that celebrity worship is nothing new.

_____

2

12. **In your own words** explain why the scale of hero worship has made a huge jump in recent years.

_____

_____

_____

2

13. What does the word "thirst" suggest about the American attitude towards celebrity gossip?

_____

_____

2

14. Why do you think the writer includes the information about the quest in Paragraph 14?

_____

_____

2

Look at Paragraphs 15 to 18.

15. What has helped to spread celebrity gossip at great speed?

_____

2

Marks

16. **In your own words** what is the "celebrity attitude scale" designed to reveal?

_____

_____   2 | 1 | 0

Look at Paragraphs 19 and 20.

17. In what **two** ways does the writer show the extent of celebrity "addiction"?   2 | 1 | 0

   (i) _____

   (ii) _____

Look at Paragraphs 21 to 24.

18. Why does the writer put the word "BUT" in capital letters at the beginning of Paragraph 21?

_____

_____   2 | 1 | 0

19. In the opinion of Francisco Gil-White, what important influence have celebrities replaced?

_____   2 | ■ | 0

20. What does the writer's use of the expression "blazing a trail" (Paragraph 24) tell you about Gareth Gates and Tiger Woods?

_____

_____   2 | ■ | 0

[Turn over for Questions 21, 22 and 23 on *Page six*

PAGE
TOTAL

Mar

Look at Paragraphs 25 to 28.

21. **In your own words** what, according to Maltby, could be the positive outcomes of admiring David Beckham?

_____

_____

2 1

22. According to Mark Griffiths:

(*a*) how can idols form a healthy part of people's lives?

Answer in your own words.

_____

_____

2 ▪

(*b*) why have pop stars and film stars replaced political and religious leaders?

Tick (✓) the appropriate box.

They are good looking. ☐

They are easily recognised. ☐

They are respected and highly regarded. ☐

2 ▪

Think about the passage as a whole.

23. "DAZZLED BY THE STARS"

Explain why, in your opinion, this is an **appropriate** title.

_____

_____

_____

2 1

[*END OF QUESTION PAPER*]

FOR OFFICIAL USE

p2	
p3	
p4	
p5	
p6	
TOTAL MARK	

[BLANK PAGE]

[BLANK PAGE]

C

0860/405

NATIONAL
QUALIFICATIONS
2005

WEDNESDAY, 4 MAY
2.30 PM – 3.20 PM

ENGLISH
STANDARD GRADE
Credit Level
Reading
Text

Read carefully the passage overleaf. It will help if you read it twice. When you have done so, answer the questions. Use the spaces provided in the Question/Answer booklet.

SCOTTISH
QUALIFICATIONS
AUTHORITY

©

1   Rameses I Station, usually called Cairo Railway Station, is a century old, like the railway system itself, which stretches from Alexandria on the shores of the Mediterranean, to Aswan on the Upper Nile, at the northern edge of Lake Nasser—the border of Sudan on the south side. The design of the station is of interest, and it has been said that it represents the epitome of nineteenth-century Egyptian architects' desire to combine classical and Islamic building styles, in response to Khedive Ismail's plan to create a "European Cairo"—Moorish meets modern.

2   Kings, queens, princes, heads of state, and generals have arrived and departed here. One of Naguib Mahfouz's earliest heroes, the ultra-nationalist anti-British rabble rouser, Saad Zaghlul, escaped an assassination attempt at Cairo Station on his return from one of his numerous exiles, in 1924. Given Egypt's history of dramatic arrivals and departures the railway station figures as a focal point and a scene of many riotous send-offs and welcomes.

3   The best story about Cairo Railway Station, told to me by a man who witnessed it unfold, does not concern a luminary but rather a person delayed in the third class ticket queue. When this fussed and furious man at last got to the window he expressed his exasperation to the clerk, saying, "Do you know who I am?"

4   The clerk looked him up and down and, without missing a beat, said, "In that shabby suit, with a watermelon under your arm, and a Third Class ticket to El Minya, who could you possibly be?"

5   To leave the enormous sprawling dust-blown city of gridlock and gritty buildings in the sleeper to Aswan was bliss. It was quarter to eight on a chilly night. I sat down in my inexpensive First Class compartment, listened to the departure whistles, and soon we were rolling through Cairo. Within minutes we were at Gizeh—the ruins overwhelmed by the traffic and the bright lights, the tenements and bazaar; and in less than half an hour we were in open country, little settlements of square mud-block houses, fluorescent lights reflected in the canal beside the track, the blackness of the countryside at night, a mosque with a lighted minaret, now and then a solitary car or truck, and on one remote road about twenty men in white robes going home after prayers. In Cairo they would have been unremarkable, just part of the mob; here they looked magical, their robes seeming much whiter on the nighttime road, their procession much spookier for its orderliness, like a troop of sorcerers.

6   I went into the corridor and opened the train window to see the robed men better, and there I was joined by Walter Frakes from St Louis, an enormous man with a long mild face, and a smooth bag-like chin, who found his compartment small, "but what's the use of fussing?" He was travelling with his wife, Marylou, and another couple, the Norrises, Lenny and Marge, also from St Louis. They too were heading to Aswan to meet a boat and take a river cruise.

7   "And if I don't get a decent bed on that ship I'm going to be a wreck," Walter Frakes said. He was a very gentle man in spite of his size, which I took to be close to 300 pounds; and he was kindly and generally uncomplaining. All he said in the morning was: "Didn't get a wink of sleep. Tried to. Woke up every time the train stopped. Must have stopped a hundred times. Durn."

8   I had woken now and then as the train had slowed at crossings, or at the larger stations. There were sometimes flaring lights, barking dogs, otherwise the silence and the darkness of the Nile Valley, and a great emptiness: the vast and starry sky of the Egyptian desert, and that road south that ran alongside the train, the only road south, *the road to Johannesburg*.

9   In the bright early morning I saw a sign saying, *Kom-Ombo - 8 km*, indicating the direction to its lovely temple with a dual dedication, to Horus, the hawk-headed god, and Sobek, the croc-skulled deity. Another sign said, *Abu Simbel Macaroni*, and depicted its glutinous product in a red bowl.

10   Date palms in clusters, orange trees, low boxy houses, donkey carts piled high with tomatoes, the occasional camel, the men in white gowns and skullcaps, the boys walking to the fields carrying farm implements, and the wide slow river and the flat bright land shimmering under the blue sky. This was new Egypt but it was also old Egypt, for I had seen many of these images in the Cairo Museum—the adzes and mattocks the boys carried I had seen looking much the same, and the same heavy browed bullocks I had seen hammered in gold or carved in stone I saw browsing by the river; the same dogs with upright tails and big ears, the same narrow cats, and had I seen a snake or a croc they would have had counterparts in gold on a chariot or else mummified and mouldering in a museum case.

11   Some of those cap and gowned men were seated in groups eating pieces of bread loaves the same shape I had seen in the museum removed intact, solid and stale, from ancient tombs; the same fava beans that had been disinterred from crypts were being gobbled up from wagons of men selling *foul*, the stewed beans that are still an Egyptian staple. The same-shaped ewers and pitchers and bowls I had seen as old artefacts were visible here in the hands of women faffing around at the kitchen doors of their huts.

12   The Nile was near, about 300 yards from bank to bank, slow moving and light brown, showing clouds on its surface, with green fields on either side, some with marked-out plots and others divided into date plantations, hawks drifting over them on the wind currents, and in the river feluccas with sails—impossible to see these sails and not think of gulls' wings. And then, as though indicating we were approaching a populous place, there was a succession of cemeteries, great long slopes of sun-baked graves, and the grave markers, small rectangles set into the stony ground, with raised edges, like a whole hillside of truckle beds where the dead people lay. Beyond the next hill was Aswan.

Adapted from *Dark Star Safari* by Paul Theroux

[END OF PASSAGE]

FOR OFFICIAL USE

C

Total
Mark

0860/406

NATIONAL
QUALIFICATIONS
2005

WEDNESDAY, 4 MAY
2.30 PM – 3.20 PM

**ENGLISH
STANDARD GRADE**
Credit Level
Reading
Questions

Fill in these boxes and read what is printed below.

Full name of centre

Town

Forename(s)

Surname

Date of birth
Day Month Year

Scottish candidate number

Number of seat

**NB Before leaving the examination room you must give this booklet to the invigilator.
If you do not, you may lose all the marks for this paper.**

SCOTTISH
QUALIFICATIONS
AUTHORITY

SAB 0860/406 6/43370

QUESTIONS

Write your answers in the spaces provided.

Look at Paragraphs 1 and 2.

1. In your own words, what do Rameses I Station and the railway system have in common?

_____ **2**

2. Why, in your opinion, does the writer use a long opening sentence?

_____ **2**

3. Quote **one** word from Paragraph 1 which clearly indicates that the station is everything which nineteenth-century Egyptian architects believed in.

┌─────────────────────────────┐
│   │
└─────────────────────────────┘ **2**

4. "Moorish meets modern."

Comment on the effectiveness of this expression.

_____

_____ **2 1**

5. How do the structure and word choice of the opening sentence of Paragraph 2 help to convey the importance of Cairo Station?

_____

_____ **2 1**

6. Quote **two expressions** from Paragraph 2 which help to convey the idea of Cairo Station's dramatic history. **2 1**

    (i) _____

    (ii) _____

Marks

Look at Paragraphs 3 and 4.

7. In your own words, explain what is surprising about the best story the writer has heard about Cairo Railway Station.

_____

_____ 2 ■ 0

Look at Paragraph 5.

8. Quote **one** word from Paragraph 5 which sums up the writer's feelings on leaving Cairo.

[   ]

2 ■ 0

9. In your own words, give **two** contrasts the writer notices on his journey from Cairo to the Egyptian countryside.

2 1 0

(i) _____

(ii) _____

10. "like a troop of sorcerers" (Paragraph 5).

Explain the effectiveness of this simile.

_____

_____ 2 1 0

Look at Paragraphs 6 to 9.

11. The writer describes Walter Frakes as kindly and generally uncomplaining.

How does he illustrate this in Paragraphs 6 and 7?

_____

_____

_____ 2 1 0

[Turn over

PAGE TOTAL

Mar

12. In your own words, how had the writer spent the overnight journey?

_____

_____ 2 1

13. Explain the different use of the italics in:

(a) "*the road to Johannesburg*" (Paragraph 8).

_____ 2

(b) "*Kom-Ombo - 8 km*" (Paragraph 9).

_____ 2

Look at Paragraphs 10 and 11.

14. What kind of impression does the writer create in the opening sentence of Paragraph 10?

_____

_____ 2 1

15. "This was new Egypt but it was also old Egypt," (Paragraph 10)

(a) In your own words, explain fully why it was possible for the writer to say this.

_____

_____ 2 1

(b) How does the writer continue this idea in Paragraph 11?

_____ 2 1

16. Explain what is unusual about the word choice in the final sentence of Paragraph 11.

_____

_____ 2 1

PAG
TOT.

Marks

Look at Paragraph 12.

17. (a) Tick (✓) the appropriate box to show which of the following statements best reflects the writer's description of the Nile.

It is muddy and polluted. ☐

It is fertile and tranquil. ☐

It is narrow and unimpressive. ☐   2 ■ 0

(b) Justify your choice with close reference to the paragraph.

_____

_____

_____   2 1 0

18. Why might the sails on the boats make the writer think of gulls' wings? Give **two** reasons.   2 1 0

(i) _____

(ii) _____

19. (a) What effect does the writer create in the final sentence of the passage?

_____

_____   2 ■ 0

(b) How does the writer create this effect?

_____

_____

_____   2 1 0

[Turn over for Question 20 on *Page six*

Mar

Think about the passage as a whole.

20. The writer of the passage is someone who has an interest in both **history** and **travel**. With close reference to the passage show how he has conveyed this to the reader.

History _____

_____

_____   2 | 1

Travel _____

_____

_____   2 | 1

[END OF QUESTION PAPER]

PAG
TOT

FOR OFFICIAL USE

p2	☐
p3	☐
p4	☐
p5	☐
p6	☐
TOTAL MARK	☐

FOR OFFICIAL USE

[BLANK PAGE]

[BLANK PAGE]

[BLANK PAGE]

F G C

0860/407

NATIONAL
QUALIFICATIONS
2003

TUESDAY, 6 MAY
9.00 AM – 10.15 AM

ENGLISH
STANDARD GRADE
Foundation, General
and Credit Levels
Writing

Read This First

1   Inside this booklet, there are photographs and words.
Use them to help you when you are thinking about what to write.
Look at all the material and think about all the possibilities.

2   There are 22 assignments altogether for you to choose from.

3   Decide which assignment you are going to attempt.
Choose only **one** and write its number in the margin of your answer book.

4   Pay close attention to what you are asked to write.
Plan what you are going to write.
Read and check your work before you hand it in.
Any changes to your work should be made clearly.

SCOTTISH
QUALIFICATIONS
AUTHORITY

©

FIRST   **Look at the picture opposite.**
        It shows someone walking across a bridge into the fog.

NEXT   Think about a place with an eerie, mysterious atmosphere.

| WHAT YOU HAVE TO WRITE |

1. **Write a story** using the following opening.

   Jan squared her shoulders and steeled herself against the biting cold. Staring ahead intently, she strode off into the chill fog . . .

   OR

2. Sometimes in darkest winter, all we want to do is huddle up in front of the fire and . . .

   Write about a special memory of such an occasion.

   You should include your **thoughts and feelings.**

   OR

3. **Write in any way you choose** using the picture opposite as your inspiration.

   OR

4. **Write a short story** using **ONE** of the following titles:

   The Stranger   The Fog   Into the Darkness

[Turn over

FIRST **Look at the picture opposite.
It shows a spider's web.**

NEXT Think about feeling trapped or being in danger.

WHAT YOU HAVE TO WRITE

5. **Write about an incident** in your life when you felt that there was no escape.

   Remember to include your **thoughts and feelings.**

   OR

6. **Write in any way you choose** using **ONE** of the following titles:

   The Web Trapped The Net

   OR

7. The natural world is in danger if we do not take steps to protect it.

   Write your views.

[Turn over

FIRST **Look at the picture opposite.**
It shows a picture of a fantasy hero.

NEXT Think about action heroes/heroines.

WHAT YOU HAVE TO WRITE

---

8. Fantasy heroes/heroines make good role models for the young.

   Write your views.

   OR

9. Write about a time when you felt that your actions were heroic.
   Remember to include your **thoughts and feelings.**

   OR

10. Violence on the screen encourages violence in real life.
    Discuss.

    OR

11. **Write a short story** using the title:
    The Warrior.

[Turn over

FIRST **Look at the picture opposite.**
It shows a CCTV camera sign.

NEXT Think about your privacy.

WHAT YOU HAVE TO WRITE

12. CCTV cameras and curfews are effective but unpopular methods of cutting crime.

    Discuss.

    OR

13. Write about an occasion in your life when you were caught doing something wrong.

    Remember to include your **thoughts and feelings.**

    OR

14. **Write a short story** using the following title:

    Caught on Camera.

[Turn over

FIRST **Look at the picture opposite.**
It shows a wave crashing against a sea wall.

NEXT Think about the power of nature.

WHAT YOU HAVE TO WRITE

---

15. Write about a time when you were caught in bad weather.

    You should include your **thoughts and feelings.**

    OR

16. Winters get windier; summers get wetter.

    Write about your views on our changing climate.

    OR

17. **Write a short story** using **ONE** of the following titles:

    The Storm   The Force

    OR

18. Storm Damage Widespread.

    Write a newspaper report using this headline.

    [Turn over for assignments 19 to 22 on *Page twelve*

There are no pictures for these assignments.

Describe the scene brought to mind by **ONE** of the following:

19. "A ship is floating in the harbour now,

    A wind is hovering o'er the mountain's brow . . ."

    P B Shelley

    OR

    "The woods are lovely, dark and deep . . ."

    Robert Frost

    OR

    "All shod with steel

    We hissed along the polished ice . . ."

    William Wordsworth

    OR

20. My Ideal Webpage.

    What features would you include in your ideal webpage and why?

    OR

21. Today we have too many rights and not enough responsibilities.

    Do you agree or disagree?

    Write your views.

    OR

22. **Write a short story** entitled:

    The Attic.

[END OF QUESTION PAPER]

[BLANK PAGE]

F
G
C

0860/407

NATIONAL QUALIFICATIONS 2004	WEDNESDAY, 5 MAY 9.00 AM – 10.15 AM	ENGLISH STANDARD GRADE Foundation, General and Credit Levels Writing

Read This First

1 Inside this booklet, there are photographs and words.
   Use them to help you when you are thinking about what to write.
   Look at all the material and think about all the possibilities.

2 There are 22 assignments altogether for you to choose from.

3 Decide which assignment you are going to attempt.
   Choose only **one** and write its number in the margin of your answer book.

4 Pay close attention to what you are asked to write.
   Plan what you are going to write.
   Read and check your work before you hand it in.
   Any changes to your work should be made clearly.

SCOTTISH QUALIFICATIONS AUTHORITY

©

FIRST   **Look at the picture opposite.**
It shows a picture of a communications satellite.

NEXT   Think about the advantages and disadvantages of communications technology.

WHAT YOU HAVE TO WRITE

1. The more television channels there are, the harder it is to find something good to watch.

   Do you agree or disagree?

   Give your views.

   OR

2. **Write a short story** in which a mobile phone plays an important part.

   OR

3. The Internet continues to make the world smaller.

   Write about the **advantages and disadvantages** of the Internet.

[Turn over

Page four

FIRST   **Look at the pictures opposite.**
         They show a young woman staring over mountain peaks,
         and a city scene.

NEXT   Think about special places you have visited.

WHAT YOU HAVE TO WRITE

4. **Write about** whether you would prefer to live in the city or the country.

   Give reasons for your choice.

   OR

5. **Write in any way you choose** using **one or both** of the pictures as your inspiration.

   OR

6. A view I will always remember.

   Write about a place which had this effect on you.

   OR

7. **Write a short story** with the title:

   No Time to Spare

   [Turn over

FIRST **Look at the picture opposite.**
It shows a student looking through the hub of a wheel.

NEXT Think about the world of work.

| WHAT YOU HAVE TO WRITE |

8. **Write an informative article** for your school magazine on a career which you want to follow when you leave school.

   OR

9. In our everyday lives we depend too much on machines.

   Discuss.

   OR

10. **Write a letter** to a local newspaper putting the case for more education for work.

    OR

11. **Write about** an occasion in your life when teamwork was vital.

    Remember to include your **thoughts and feelings.**

[Turn over

FIRST **Look at the picture opposite.**
       It shows a young boy winning a race.

NEXT   Think about what it feels like to take part in an event.

WHAT YOU HAVE TO WRITE

---

12. **Write about** an achievement you remember above all others.

    Remember to include your **thoughts and feelings.**

    OR

13. Communities today do not have enough organised events to suit young people.

    Discuss.

    OR

14. "It is the taking part that is important, not the winning."

    Do you agree or disagree?

    Give your views.

    OR

15. **Write a short story** using the title:

    Crossing The Line

[Turn over

Page ten

FIRST **Look at the picture opposite.**
 It shows a man looking out of his house window over a city.

NEXT Think about what it feels like to be different.

WHAT YOU HAVE TO WRITE

16. **Write a short story** about a character who is isolated from society.

 OR

17. **Write in any way you choose** using **one** of the following titles:

 Keeper of the City Success The Glass House

 OR

18. **Write a description** of your ideal home.

 OR

19. Even famous people have a right to privacy.

 Do you agree or disagree?

 Give your views.

 [Turn over for assignments 20 to 22 on *Page twelve*

There are no pictures for these assignments.

20. "Shop till you drop."

   Retail therapy does more harm than good.

   Discuss.

   OR

21. **Describe the scene** brought to mind by **one** of the following:

   For winter rains and ruins are over,
   And all the season of snows

   Swinburne

   OR

   He will watch from dawn to gloom
   The lake-reflected sun

   Shelley

   OR

   The rocky summits, split and rent,
   Formed turret, dome, or battlement

   Scott

22. **Write a short story** using the title:

   Appearances Can Be Deceptive

[END OF QUESTION PAPER]

[BLANK PAGE]

F
G
C

0860/407

NATIONAL
QUALIFICATIONS
2005

WEDNESDAY, 4 MAY
9.00 AM – 10.15 AM

ENGLISH
STANDARD GRADE
Foundation, General
and Credit Levels
Writing

Read This First

1 Inside this booklet, there are photographs and words.
Use them to help you when you are thinking about what to write.
Look at all the material and think about all the possibilities.

2 There are 23 assignments altogether for you to choose from.

3 Decide which assignment you are going to attempt.
Choose only **one** and write its number in the margin of your answer book.

4 Pay close attention to what you are asked to write.
Plan what you are going to write.
Read and check your work before you hand it in.
Any changes to your work should be made clearly.

SCOTTISH
QUALIFICATIONS
AUTHORITY

©

FIRST   **Look at the picture opposite.
It shows a holiday scene.**

NEXT   Think about holidays.

| WHAT YOU HAVE TO WRITE |

1. Even the worst holiday can have its funny side.

   Write about your experience of a holiday like this.

   Remember to include your **thoughts and feelings**.

   OR

2. **Write an article for a magazine describing** your favourite holiday resort and outlining its main attractions.

   OR

3. Sun, sea and sand.

   Surely there must be more to a holiday than that?

   Do you agree or disagree? Give your views.

   OR

4. **Write a short story** entitled:

   Going Places.

[Turn over

FIRST   **Look at the picture opposite.**
         It shows a train in a station at night.

NEXT   Think about journeys by train.

WHAT YOU HAVE TO WRITE

5. **Write about** a memorable train journey.

   Remember to include your **thoughts and feelings.**

   OR

6. Trains and railways are fascinating but can be dangerous.

   Discuss.

   OR

7. **Write a short story** using **ONE** of the following titles:

   Night Train   The Deserted Station   Crossing The Border

   OR

8. Trainspotting—an unusual hobby?

   Do you have a hobby which some people might consider unusual?

   Write about it, making it clear why **you** enjoy it.

[Turn over

FIRST   **Look at the picture opposite.
It shows a father coaching his son.**

NEXT   Think about competitive sport.

WHAT YOU HAVE TO WRITE

---

9.   Young people today are under too much pressure to succeed.

     Do you agree or disagree? Give your views.

     OR

10.   **Write about** an occasion when you took part in a sporting activity and lost.

     Remember to include your **thoughts and feelings.**

     OR

11.   **Write a short story** entitled:

     Determination.

     OR

12.   Playing in a team has much more to offer than competing as an individual.

     Do you agree or disagree? Give your views.

[Turn over

FIRST   **Look at the picture opposite.
          It shows an iceberg.**

NEXT   Think about the beauty and danger of icebergs.

WHAT YOU HAVE TO WRITE

---

13. **Write in any way you choose** using the picture opposite as your inspiration.

    OR

14. **Write a newspaper article** using the headline:

    Ship Strikes Iceberg!

    OR

15. Global warming will end us if we do not end it.

    Do you agree or disagree? Give your views.

    OR

16. **Write a short story** using **ONE** of the following titles:

    Iceworld   Hidden Depths

[Turn over

FIRST **Look at the pictures opposite.**
They show amateur and professional performers.

NEXT Think about live performance.

| WHAT YOU HAVE TO WRITE |

17. **Write about** an occasion when you
    either took part in a live performance
    or helped behind the scenes.
    Remember to include your **thoughts and feelings.**

    OR

18. Television shows such as *Pop Idol* do more harm than good.
    Discuss.

    OR

19. **Write a short story** using **ONE** of the following titles:
    The Fame Game   Practice Makes Perfect

[Turn over for assignments 20 to 23 on *Page twelve*

There are no pictures for these assignments.

20. **Write a letter** using the following opening.

    Dear Sir/Madam,

    I am writing to complain in the strongest possible terms about . . .

OR

21. **Describe the scene** brought to mind by the following:

    "Scarring the very sky, they scrape and scratch ever upwards, those rectangles of glass and stone—our so modern office blocks."

OR

22. Letter-writing today is not dead; it has simply been updated by e-mail, texting and messaging.

    Discuss.

OR

23. **Write a short story** using **ONE** of the following openings.

    Make sure that you develop **character** and **setting** as well as **plot**.

    A cruel smile played on Kane's lips as he swung open the heavy door and stepped out into the cold, grim world . . .

    OR

    It was a misty morning in late November and Jane was late. Frantically late. She quickened her step . . .

    OR

    Tom was puzzled. Well, perhaps more perplexed than puzzled. He sat staring, wide-eyed, at the letter on the table . . .

[END OF QUESTION PAPER]

[BLANK PAGE]

[BLANK PAGE]

[BLANK PAGE]

Acknowledgements

Leckie & Leckie is grateful to the copyright holders, as credited, for permission to use their material:

John Donald Publishers (Birlinn) Ltd for the short story 'An Invisible Man' by Brian McCabe, originally published in *The Macallan/Scotland on Sunday collection of Short Stories* (2002 Credit Reading paper pp 2–4);

'We're out for the Count' by Catriona Marchant © *The Times*, London, 13 October 2001 (2003 General Reading paper p 2);

Express Newspapers for the article 'Why the Dodo is dead' by Alex West (2003 Credit Reading paper p 2);

Allstar Picture Library for a photograph (2003 Writing paper p 6);

The Mail on Sunday for the article 'Pucker way to kiss a hummingbird' by Mark Carwardine (2004 General Reading paper p 2);

The BBC for a photograph (2004 General Reading paper p 2);

Getty Images for a photograph (2004 Writing paper p 2);

Getty Images for a photograph (2004 Writing paper p 8);

Camera Press, London, for a photograph by John Swannell (2004 Writing paper p 10);

The Sunday Times for the article 'Dazzling the Stars' by John Harlow (2005 General Reading paper p 2);

FreeFoto.com for a photograph (2005 Writing paper p 4);

The Scotsman for a photograph (2005 Writing paper p 6);

Ralph A. Clevenger/Corbis for a photograph (2005 Writing paper p 8).

The following companies/individuals have very generously given permission to reproduce their copyright material free of charge:

Catherine Czerkawska for an article from *The Scotsman* (2001 General Reading paper p 2);

Curtis Brown for an extract from *Watching Mrs Gordon and Other Stories* by Ronald Frame (2001 Credit Reading paper pp 2–4):

Michael Munro for an extract from *Application* (2002 General Reading paper pp 2–3);

FreeFoto.com for 4 photographs (2003 Writing paper pp 2, 4, 8 &10);

Captain Corelli's Mandolin by Louis de Berniéres, published by Martin Secker & Warburg. Reprinted by permission of The Random House Group. (2004 Credit Reading paper pp 2–3);

Maurice Lacroix Ltd for an advertisement (2004 Writing paper p 4);

Newsquest Media Group for a photograph (2004 Writing paper p 4);

News Team International for a photograph (2004 Writing paper p 6);

Dark Star Safari: Overland from Cairo to Cape Town by Paul Theroux (Penguin Books 2002). Copyright © Cape Cod Scriveners Co. 2002. Reproduced by permission of Penguin Books Ltd. (2005 Credit Reading paper pp 2–3);

Newsquest Media Group for a photograph (2005 Writing paper p 10);

TES Scotland for a photograph (2005 Writing paper p 10).

English Writing—2003 to 2005

	Credit	General	Foundation
	The work displays some distinction in ideas, construction and language. This is shown by a detailed attention to the purposes of the writing task; by qualities such as knowledge, insight, imagination; and by development that is sustained. Vocabulary, paragraphing and sentence construction are accurate and varied.	The work shows a general awareness of the purposes of the writing task. It has a number of appropriate ideas and evidence of structure. Vocabulary is on the whole accurate, but lacks variety.	The work shows a few signs of appropriateness and commitment to the purposes of the writing task.
As the task requires. The candidate can	convey information, selecting and highlighting what is most significant;	convey information in some kind of sequence;	convey simple information;
	marshall ideas and evidence in support of an argument; these ideas have depth and some complexity; he/she is capable of objectivity, generalisation and evaluation;	order and present ideas and opinions with an attempt at reasoning;	present ideas and opinions in concrete personal terms;
	give a succinct account of a personal experience: the writing has insight and self-awareness;	give a reasonably clear account of a personal experience with some sense of involvement;	convey the gist of a personal experience;
	express personal feelings and reactions sensitively;	express personal feelings and reactions with some attempt to go beyond bald statement;	make a bald statement of personal feelings or reactions;
	display some skills in using the conventions of a chosen literary form, and in manipulating language to achieve particular effects.	use some of the more obvious conventions of a chosen literary form, and occasionally use language to achieve particular effects.	display a rudimentary awareness of the more obvious conventions of a chosen literary form, and occasionally attempt to use language to achieve particular effects.

A combination of these qualities may be called for by any one writing task.

	Credit	General	Foundation
Intelligibility and Correctness	Writing which the candidate submits as finished work communicates meaning clearly at a first reading. Sentence construction is accurate and formal errors will not be significant.	Writing which the candidate submits as finished work communicates meaning at first reading. There are some lapses in punctuation, spelling and sentence construction.	Writing which the candidate submits as finished work communicates meaning largely at first reading: however, some further reading is necessary because of obtrusive formal errors and/or structural weaknesses, including inaccurate sentence construction and poor vocabulary.
Length	When it is appropriate to do so, the candidate can sustain the quality of writing at some length. Pieces of extended writing submitted in the folio of coursework should not normally exceed 800 words in length. The overriding consideration is, however, that the length should be appropriate to the purposes of the writing task.	Length is appropriate to the purposes of the writing task.	100 words is to be taken as a rough guide to the minimum length expected for each finished piece of work, but the overriding consideration should be that the length is appropriate to the purposes of the writing task.

	Grade 1	Grade 2	Grade 3	Grade 4	Grade 5	Grade 6
Differentiating Factors	The finished communication is not only clear; it is also stylish. Attention to purpose is not only detailed; it is also sensitive. Writing shows overall distinction in ideas, construction and language. Vocabulary is apt and extensive, and paragraphing and sentence construction are skilful. In these respects performance transcends the level of accuracy and variety acceptable at grade 2.	Evidence of one or more of the qualities of distinction in ideas, construction or language is present but these qualities are less well sustained and/or combined than at grade 1. In the main writing is substantial, accurate and relevant, but it lacks the insight, economy and style which characterises achievement at grade 1.	Writing is characterised by overall adequacy of communication. It conveys its meaning clearly and sentence construction and paragraphing are on the whole accurate. There is a reasonably sustained attention to purpose, and structure shows some coherence. Where appropriate there is a measure of generalisation and objectivity in reasoning.	Writing approaches the qualities of adequacy required for grade 3 but is clearly seen to be impaired in one of the following ways: there are significant inaccuracies in sentence construction. or the work is thin in appropriate ideas. or the work is weak in structure.	Writing rises a little above basic intelligibility and rudimentary attention to purpose. Formal errors and weaknesses are obtrusive but not as numerous as at grade 6. Attention to the purposes of the writing task is weak but the quality of the writer's ideas is perceptibly stronger than at grade 6.	Writing contains many formal errors and structural weaknesses but they do not overall have the effect of baffling the reader. The conveying of simple information is marked by obscurities and extraneous detail, and the presentation of ideas, opinions and personal experience is somewhat rambling and disjointed.

English Writing—2003

Narrative Numbers 1, 4, 11, 14, 17, 22

Task specifications/rubric/purposes

The criteria demand appropriate ideas and evidence of structure which in the narrative genre involve **plot** or **content** or **atmosphere**.

No 1	short story -	**imposed opening** must be used.
No 4	short story -	one of the three imposed titles must be reflected in the narrative. **The Stranger**. **The Fog**. **Into The Darkness**.
No 11	short story -	imposed title **The Warrior** must be evident in the narrative.
No 14	short story -	imposed title **Caught On Camera** must be reflected in the narrative.
No 17	short story -	**one** of the two imposed titles must be used. **The Storm**. **The Force**.
No 22	short story -	imposed title **The Attic** must feature in the narrative.

Grade Differentiation

1:2   Grade 1 narrative will show **overall distinction** in IDEAS, CONSTRUCTION and LANGUAGE, and will be both **stylish** and **skilful**, while Grade 2 narrative will fall short both in the quality and in the **combination** of skills.

3:4   Grade 3 responses will have an **appropriate plot**, will make use of appropriate **register** to create ATMOSPHERE or SUSPENSE and should include NARRATIVE or DESCRIPTIVE details to establish the main lines of the plot. Do not forget that lack of variety in plot and language skills is typical of Grade 3. Accuracy is the criterion to establish here.

Grade 4's **simple plot** will approach the adequacy of Grade 3 but may be poorly organised or have significant inaccuracies.

5:6   Grade 5's **very basic plot** will occasionally try to achieve particular effects, and it will also be poorly organised and have significant inaccuracies.

Grade 6 will have a combination of negative features, will be **rambling**, or have **obscurities** in the plot and the marker will have difficulty in decoding because of very poor spelling, sentencing, or handwriting.

NB   If candidates ignore the rubric in respect of plot or character this may place them in Grade 5 in terms of purpose ('few signs of appropriateness'), unless there are other strong compensating features ('accurate', 'varied', 'sensitive'). Where there are no strong compensating features, this may tip the balance overall into Grade 6.

Discursive/Informative Numbers 7, 8, 10, 12, 16, 18, 20, 21

Task specifications/rubrics/purposes

The rubrics cover controversial issues which are likely to elicit emotional responses. Objectivity is not required but clear, straightforward presentation of a point of view is required. At all levels, candidates must deal with the specific topics.

No 7   **agree/disagree or balanced view**. Candidates may choose to deal with the topic from one particular point of view or take a more balanced approach. Some background knowledge is required. The words, 'natural world,' could be interpreted widely to encompass conservation issues.

No 8   **agree/disagree or balanced view**. Personal/anecdotal evidence may feature but this should contribute to the candidate's line of thought.

No 10   **agree/disagree/balanced view** of the issue. Candidates should follow a line of argument with supporting evidence.

No 12   **agree/disagree/balanced**. Some background knowledge is required. Personal/anecdotal evidence may be present but this should follow a line of thought. Candidates must cover CCTV cameras and curfews. Mention should also be made of their lack of popularity.

No 16   **agree/disagree/balanced view**. Anecdotal evidence is likely to feature but should be used to support a line of thought. Candidates should indicate the reasons behind their opinions.

No 18   The format here is a newspaper report and the purpose of the task is clearly conveying information. Writing in columns is not essential but the features of the genre should be evident. For example, an appropriate tone should be established.

No 20   This task combines a number of writing purposes. Information is being sought and because of the nature of that information, some anecdotal material may appear. Additionally, opinions are required justifying choices made.

No 21   **agree/disagree or balanced**. Candidates may choose to deal with the topic from one particular point of view or take a more balanced approach. A clear line of thought/argument should be present with supporting evidence. Anecdotal material should contribute to the line of thought.

Grade Differentiation - Discursive

1:2   Grade 1 responses will show a **combination of depth, complexity and skilful deployment** of ideas, and will marshall evidence in support of an argument.

Grade 2 responses will lack this combination of technical skill and confident tone, presenting ideas in a **less developed** or **sustained** manner.

3:4   Grade 3 will attempt an orderly flow of ideas, which may not succeed logically, whereas Grade 4 will be typically **weak in structure**, or **have thin ideas** or **poorly constructed sentences**.

5:6   Grade 5 will present ideas and opinions in **concrete, personal terms** which may be anecdotal, but are more than a bald series of unsupported **disjointed** or **rambling** statements, the hallmarks of Grade 6.

Grade Differentiation-Informative

1:2   Grade 1 will convey information in a **clear sequence, selecting and highlighting** what is most significant. Grade 2 responses will be **less well sustained** in terms of the qualities of distinction in **ideas, construction and language**.

3:4   Grade 3 will convey the relevant information **in some kind of sequence** which may not succeed logically, whereas Grade 4 will be **weak in structure** or have **thin ideas** or **weak sentence construction**.

5:6   Grade 5 will convey only **simple information**. Formal errors will be obtrusive but the writing will not be marked by the **rambling** and **disjointed** statements which define Grade 6.

Personal Experience/Descriptive Numbers 2, 5, 9, 13, 15, 19

Task specifications/rubric/purposes

Each of the above calls for a personal response; while there are no genre requirements here, content must be specific and appropriate.

No 2   a **single occasion** should be selected by candidates. Thoughts and feelings associated with the memory should be evident.

No 5   a **single specific incident** is required. Candidates should concentrate not only on the narrative but also on associated thoughts and feelings.

No 9   the rubric restricts the candidate to a **specific occasion** when they considered their actions to be heroic. The evocation of associated thoughts and feelings is explicit in the task. A wide interpretation of the term 'heroic' is acceptable.

No 13   candidates are restricted to a **single occasion** when caught wrongdoing. The evocation of associated thoughts and feelings is explicit in the task. Mention of the consequences is acceptable. Stronger candidates may make the shift into reflective writing.

No 15   a **single occasion** is required. Candidates are free to determine the exact nature of the 'bad weather' but it should be mentioned. An element of description is also implicit in this task.

No 19   Candidates must select **one** of the three scenes and then write a description.

Grade Differentiation

1:2   Grade 1 will be a well-crafted, stylish account and will deploy a range of skills to express perceptiveness and self-awareness and to achieve or create effects, while a Grade 2 account will be soundly constructed and show a **measure of insight and self-awareness** expressed accurately. Grade 2 may not be succinct but will be **substantial**.

3:4   A Grade 3 response will be reasonably well sustained, with easily grasped structure, and will on the whole be correct but with a certain dull monotony.

Grade 4 will be structurally weak or thin in ideas but will still **attempt involvement, approaching the overall adequacy of Grade 3**.

5:6   Grade 5 may have positive features such as a runaway enthusiasm which may detract from the stated purpose but it will present the **gist** of the experience without **ramblings** and **incoherence** which, along with **numerous errors** and near-illegible handwriting are the mark of Grade 6.

English Writing—2003 (cont.)

Free Choice Numbers 3, 6

Task specifications/rubric/purposes

Each of the above calls for the candidate to determine the purpose of the writing and format. It is therefore important that the candidate's writing purpose is made clear in the course of the response. Writing should be assessed according to the appropriate criteria.

No 3   the rubric restricts the candidate to the **use of the picture** and **its associated ideas** as the stimulus for the writing piece.

No 6   the rubric restricts the candidate to **one** of the titles offered.

English Writing—2004

Narrative Numbers 2, 7, 15, 16, 22

Task specifications/rubric/purposes

The criteria demand appropriate ideas and evidence of structure which in the narrative genre involve **plot** or **content** or **atmosphere**.

No 2   short story –   a mobile phone must be clearly evident in the narrative.
No 7   short story –   imposed title **No Time to Spare** must be reflected in the narrative.
No 15   short story –   imposed title **Crossing the Line** must be reflected in the narrative.
No 16   short story –   the idea of **ONE** character being isolated must be reflected in the narrative. The word 'society' could be interpreted narrowly. ie peer group.
No 22   short story –   imposed title **Appearances Can be Deceptive** must be reflected in the narrative.

Grade Differentiation

1 : 2   Grade 1 narrative will show **overall distinction** in IDEAS, CONSTRUCTION and LANGUAGE, and will be both **stylish and skilful**, while Grade 2 narrative will fall short both in the quality and in the **combination** of skills.

3 : 4   Grade 3 responses will have an **appropriate plot**, will make use of appropriate **register** to create ATMOSPHERE or SUSPENSE and should include NARRATIVE or DESCRIPTIVE details to establish the main lines of the plot. Do not forget that lack of variety in plot and language skills is typical of Grade 3. Accuracy is the criterion to establish here.

Grade 4's **simple plot** will approach the adequacy of Grade 3 but may be poorly organised or have significant inaccuracies.

5 : 6   Grade 5's **very basic plot** will occasionally try to achieve particular effects, and it will also be poorly organised and have significant inaccuracies.

Grade 6 will have a combination of negative features, will be **rambling**, or have **obscurities** in the plot and the marker will have difficulty in decoding because of very poor spelling, sentencing, or handwriting.

NB   If candidates ignore the rubric in respect of plot or character this may place them in Grade 5 in terms of purpose ('few signs of appropriateness'), unless there are other strong compensating features ('accurate', 'varied', 'sensitive'). Where there are no strong compensating features, this may tip the balance overall into Grade 6.

Discursive/Informative Numbers 1, 3, 4, 8, 9, 10, 13, 14, 19, 20

Task specifications/rubrics/purposes

The rubrics cover controversial issues which are likely to elicit emotional responses. Objectivity is not required but clear, straightforward presentation of a point of view is required. At all levels, candidates must deal with the specific topics.

No 1   **agree/disagree or balanced view.** Candidates may choose to deal with the topic from one particular point of view or take a more balanced approach to the topic. Some background knowledge is required. Personal/anecdotal evidence may figure but should be used to support the candidate's line of argument.

No 3   both advantages and disadvantages **must** be covered as this is made explicit in the task.

No 4   either city or country **must** be chosen. Personal/anecdotal evidence is likely to feature but must be used to support a line of thought.

No 8   the main purpose is to convey information on a career choice. Personal/anecdotal evidence may appear.

No 9   **agree/disagree/balanced.** Some background knowledge is required. Personal/anecdotal evidence may be present but this should follow a line of thought.

No 10   **agree.** Imposed letter format. Some background knowledge is required. Candidates should indicate the reasons behind their opinions. Personal/anecdotal evidence may be present.

No 13   **agree/disagree or balanced.** Some personal/anecdotal evidence may be present but this should be used to support the line of thought adopted by the candidate.

English Writing—2004 (cont.)

No 14 **agree/disagree or balanced**. Some personal/anecdotal evidence may be present but this should be used to support the line of thought adopted by the candidate.

No 19 **agree/disagree or balanced**. Candidates may choose to deal with the topic from one particular point of view or take a more balanced approach to the topic. A clear line of thought/argument should be present with supporting evidence.

No 20 **agree/disagree or balanced view.** Personal/anecdotal evidence may feature heavily but this should support the line of thought adopted by the candidate.

Grade Differentiation – Discursive

1 : 2 Grade 1 responses will show a **combination of depth, complexity and skilful deployment** of ideas, and will marshall evidence in support of an argument.

Grade 2 responses will lack this combination of technical skill and confident tone, presenting ideas in a **less developed** or **sustained** manner.

3 : 4 Grade 3 will attempt an orderly flow of ideas, which may not succeed logically, whereas Grade 4 will be typically **weak in structure**, or **have thin ideas** or poorly constructed sentences.

5 : 6 Grade 5 will present ideas and opinions in **concrete, personal terms** which may be anecdotal, but are more than a bald series of unsupported **disjointed** or **rambling** statements, the hallmarks of Grade 6.

Grade Differentiation-Informative

1 : 2 Grade 1 will convey information in a **clear sequence, selecting and highlighting** what is most significant.

Grade 2 responses will be **less well sustained** in terms of the qualities of distinction in **ideas, construction and language**.

3 : 4 Grade 3 will convey the relevant information **in some kind of sequence** which may not succeed logically, whereas Grade 4 will be **weak in structure** or have **thin ideas** or **weak sentence construction.**

5 : 6 Grade 5 will convey only **simple information**. Formal errors will be obtrusive but the writing will not be marked by the **rambling** and **disjointed** statements which define Grade 6.

Personal Experience/Descriptive Numbers 6, 11, 12, 18, 21

Task specifications/rubric/purposes

Each of the above calls for a personal response; while there are no genre requirements here, content must be specific and appropriate.

No 6 a **single** specific view is required. Description of the chosen place is explicit in the rubric and candidates should concentrate not only on the narrative but also on associated thoughts and feelings.

No 11 the rubric restricts the candidate to a specific occasion when teamwork was important. The evocation of associated thoughts and feelings is explicitly required in the task.

No 12 the rubric restricts the candidate to a single achievement although other achievements may be mentioned to highlight the significance of the one chosen.

No 18 description of the characteristics of the candidate's ideal choice is required. Personal feelings and reactions should be evident.

No 21 candidates must choose one of the quotations. Description is explicit in the rubric.

Grade Differentiation

1 : 2 Grade 1 will be a well crafted, stylish account and will deploy a range of skills to express perceptiveness and self-awareness and to achieve or create effects, while a Grade 2 account will be soundly constructed and show a **measure of insight** and self-awareness expressed accurately. Grade 2 may not be succinct but will be **substantial**.

3 : 4   A Grade 3 response will be reasonably well sustained, with easily grasped structure, and will on the whole be correct but with a certain dull monotony.

         Grade 4 will be structurally weak and thin in ideas but will still **attempt involvement, approaching the overall adequacy** of Grade 3.

5 : 6   Grade 5 may have positive features such as a runaway enthusiasm which may detract from the stated purpose but it will present the **gist** of the experience without **ramblings** and **incoherence** which, along with **numerous errors** and near-illegible handwriting are the mark of Grade 6.

Free Choice Numbers   5, 17

Task specifications/rubric/purposes

Each of the above calls for the candidate to determine the purpose of the writing and format. It is therefore important that the candidate's writing purpose is made clear in the course of the response. Markers should assess according to the appropriate criteria.

No 5   the rubric restricts the candidate to **one or both** picture stimuli.

No 17   the rubric restricts the candidate to a choice of **one** of the titles offered.

English Writing—2005

Narrative Numbers 4, 7, 11, 16, 19, 23

Task specifications/rubric/purposes

The criteria demand appropriate ideas and evidence of structure which in the narrative genre involve **plot** or **content** or **atmosphere**.

No 4   Short story –   Imposed title **Going Places** must be reflected in the narrative although this title offers considerable latitude.

No 7   Short story –   Candidates must select ONE of the three options: Night Train OR The Deserted Station OR Crossing The Border. The selection should be reflected in the narrative.

No 11   Short story –   Imposed title **Determination** must be reflected in the narrative.

No 16   Short story –   Candidates must select ONE of the two options: Iceworld OR Hidden Depths. Either title may be interpreted metaphorically.

No 19   Short story –   ONE of the TWO openings must be used. The Fame Game or Practice Makes Perfect. The selection should be reflected in the narrative.

No 23   Short story –   ONE of the THREE openings must be used. Thereafter, character, setting and plot must be clearly developed from the imposed opening selected.

Grade Differentiation

1 : 2   Grade 1 narrative will show **overall distinction** in IDEAS, CONSTRUCTION and LANGUAGE, and will be both **stylish and skilful**, while Grade 2 narrative will fall short both in the quality and in the **combination** of skills.

3 : 4   Grade 3 responses will have an **appropriate plot**, will make use of appropriate **register** to create ATMOSPHERE or SUSPENSE and should include NARRATIVE or DESCRIPTIVE details to establish the main lines of the plot. Do not forget that lack of variety in plot and language skills is typical of Grade 3. Accuracy is the criterion to establish here.

Grade 4's **simple plot** will approach the adequacy of Grade 3 but may be poorly organised or have significant inaccuracies.

5 : 6   Grade 5's **very basic plot** will occasionally try to achieve particular effects, and it will also be poorly organised and have significant inaccuracies.

Grade 6 will have a combination of negative features, will be **rambling**, or have **obscurities** in the plot and the marker will have difficulty in decoding because of very poor spelling, sentencing, or handwriting.

NB   If candidates ignore the rubric in respect of plot or character this may place them in Grade 5 in terms of purpose ('a few signs of appropriateness'), unless there are other strong compensating features ('accurate', 'varied', 'sensitive'). Where there are no strong compensating features, this may tip the balance overall into Grade 6.

Discursive/Informative Numbers   2, 3, 6, 8, 9, 12, 14, 15, 18, 20, 22
Task specifications/rubrics/purposes

The rubrics cover controversial issues which are likely to elicit emotional responses. Objectivity is not required but clear, straightforward presentation of a point of view is required. At all levels, candidates must deal with the specific topics.

No 2   The main purpose is to convey information about a favourite holiday resort and its main attractions. Personal/anecdotal evidence may appear.

No 3   **Agree/disagree/balanced**. Personal/anecdotal evidence may well feature.

No 6   The ideas of both attraction and danger should be covered. Personal/anecdotal evidence should be used to progress a line of thought.

No 8   The main purpose is to convey information on what the candidate enjoys about an unusual hobby. This piece has both W1 and W3 elements ie conveying information and personal experience. The term 'unusual' should be interpreted liberally.

No 9   **Agree/disagree/balanced**. Personal/ anecdotal evidence may be present but this should follow a line of thought.

No 12   **Agree/disagree/balanced**. Candidates should indicate the reasons behind their opinions. Personal/anecdotal evidence may be present.

No 14   The main purpose is to convey information in the form of a newspaper report.

No 15   **Agree/disagree or balanced.** Some background knowledge is required. Personal/anecdotal evidence should be used to support a line of thought.

No 18   **Agree/ disagree or balanced.** Candidates may choose to deal with the topic from one particular point of view or take a more balanced approach to the topic. A clear line of thought/argument should be present with supporting evidence. Any response on the 'reality tv' theme should be considered to be appropriate.

No 20   Imposed opening. Candidates are left free to choose the context for the letter of complaint.

No 22   **Agree/disagree or balanced view.** Personal/anecdotal evidence is likely to feature here and is entirely acceptable.

Grade Differentiation – Discursive

1 : 2   Grade 1 responses will show a **combination of depth, complexity** and **skilful deployment** of ideas, and will marshall evidence in support of an argument.

       Grade 2 responses will lack this combination of technical skill and confident tone, presenting ideas in a **less developed** or **sustained manner.**

3 : 4   Grade 3 will attempt an orderly flow of ideas, which may not succeed logically, whereas Grade 4 will be typically **weak in structure**, or **have thin ideas** or poorly constructed sentences.

5 : 6   Grade 5 will present ideas and opinions in **concrete, personal terms** which may be anecdotal, but are more than a bald series of unsupported **disjointed** or **rambling statements**, the hallmarks of Grade 6.

Grade Differentiation-Informative

1 : 2   Grade 1 will convey information in a **clear sequence, selecting and highlighting** what is most significant. Grade 2 responses will be **less well sustained** in terms of the qualities of distinction in **ideas, construction and language.**

3 : 4   Grade 3 will convey the relevant information **in some kind of sequence** which may not succeed logically, whereas Grade 4 will be **weak in structure** or have **thin ideas** or **weak sentence construction.**

5 : 6   Grade 5 will convey only **simple information.** Formal errors will be obtrusive but the writing will not be marked by the **rambling** and **disjointed** statements which define Grade 6.

Personal Experience/Descriptive Numbers   1, 5, 10, 17, 21

Task specifications/rubric/purposes

Each of the above calls for a personal response; while there are no genre requirements here, content must be specific and appropriate.

No 1   A **single** holiday should be chosen although candidates may cover a range of experiences within the chosen holiday. Candidates should concentrate not only on the narrative but also on associated thoughts and feelings.

No 5   The rubric restricts the candidate to a specific and 'memorable' train journey. The evocation of associated thoughts and feelings is explicitly required in the task.

No 10   The rubric restricts the candidate to a single sporting activity which is ultimately unsuccessful. The evocation of thoughts and feelings should be evident.

No 17   The rubric restricts the candidate to a single occasion where they either took part in a live performance or helped out. Personal feelings and reactions should be evident.

No 21   Candidates should write a description of the scene **suggested** by the quotation.

English Writing - 2005 (Cont.)

Grade Differentiation

1 : 2 Grade 1 will be a well crafted, stylish account and will deploy a range of skills to express perceptiveness and self-awareness and to achieve or create effects, while a Grade 2 account will be soundly constructed and show a **measure of insight** and self-awareness expressed accurately. Grade 2 may not be succinct but will be **substantial**.

3 : 4 A Grade 3 response will be reasonably well sustained, with easily grasped structure, and will on the whole be correct but with a certain dull monotony.

Grade 4 will be structurally weak and thin in ideas but will still **attempt involvement, approaching the overall adequacy** of Grade 3.

5 : 6 Grade 5 may have positive features such as a runaway enthusiasm which may detract from the stated purpose but it will present the **gist** of the experience without **ramblings** and **incoherence** which, along with **numerous errors** and near-illegible handwriting are the markers of Grade 6.

Free Choice Number   13

Task specifications/rubric/purposes

Each of the above calls for the candidate to determine the purpose of the writing and format. It is therefore important that the candidate's writing purpose is made clear in the course of the response. Markers should assess according to the appropriate criteria.

No 13 The rubric restricts the candidate to the picture stimulus.

English General Level
Reading 2001

1. Reference to any TWO of—use of colon (to introduce)/(a list of) examples/unwanted gifts/wee something for Christmas/birthday gift not wanted/holiday souvenirs/stuff/(which) clutters our lives/recycled rubbish

2. bizarre
   store

3. (i) *Occasional*
       on a temporary site (eg rented/hired for the day)
   (ii) *Regular*
       on a (more) permanent site

4. (*a*) . . . retire shyly . . .
   (*b*) She finds it surprising/odd/ strange/puzzling

5. (*a*) (i) because he tells jokes which you're forced to listen to/which are not funny/which are offensive
       (ii) because they buy things of which their wives will disapprove
   (*b*) She involves the reader by use of an informal, chatty tone/sense of immediacy OR She creates an image of a succession of people by repetition

6. **In your own words**
   You have to beware of dodgy dealers OR Official organisations may be involved because of illegal activities.

7. (*a*) (i) fakes (ii) stolen goods
       (iii) (cheap or dodgy) cigarettes
   (*b*) That it might not have been prepared properly/healthily

8. (. . . on the whole . . .) they have little trouble OR Most are legitimate and harmless

9. Each is structured as a command. OR Each begins with an imperative/a verb/a word which tells or advises you what to do

10. (*a*) . . . like wild dogs around a carcase . . .
    (*b*) It conveys effectively how they fight/compete over their share/over the best bits

11. **In your own words**
    (*a*) There would be too much stuff for it provides more space than the boot of a car
    (*b*) To help you look after things while you have a break

12. **Any two**
    Boxes—rickety or broken/baseball caps—free to start with/plastic dinosaurs—used or damaged/ tattie-peeler—difficult to wash/plastic containers—ill-fitting lids/pancake mixer—splashes
    Any two

13. **In your own words**
    You can get rid of a lot of unwanted objects/ contribute to other people's happiness/see lots of different people/make a little money
    Any two

14. It is difficult to resist (the temptation of) buying OR the idea of one person's junk being valuable to others.

15. To show that the list could continue/be endless OR that there could be more examples

16. (i) (wall-papering) table/people are well wrapped-up/there's a friend to help out
    (ii) electrical goods are on sale

17. Any choice is acceptable, but should be supported:
    information—lots of facts/advice given + appropriate reference
    entertainment—humorous tone + appropriate reference
    thought-provoking—provides advice/reflection + appropriate reference

English Credit Level
Reading 2001

1. **In your own words**

   The visit had been planned many times (in the past) but had never taken place

2. Their arrival
   by taxi

3. (a) She was meeting visitors they'd never seen before

   (b) She stated the obvious/spoke unnecessarily

4. (a) She is controlled/precise/deliberate/calculating/elegant/contrived/graceful/attention-seeking/self-conscious (eg show-off/poser)

   Any one

   (b) She is wealthy OR strange/unusual/extraordinary/different OR bold/self-confident/exotic

   Any one

5. Parenthesis
   (or appropriate explanation eg to provide extra or additional information)

6. (a) She was surprised/taken aback/disapproving/envious/intimidated

   Any one

   (b) The number and colour of the suitcases

7. **In your own words**

   She had felt offended/insulted/aggrieved (by the aunt's comments) but was too polite to say so/but wanted to put the aunt in her place/but realised the aunt was not being offensive

8. (a) Shy/retiring/lacking confidence/nervous

   Any one

   (b) Reference to him as a "shadow" (Paragraph 7) meaning that he is in the background

9. **In your own words**

   (a) He welcomed them in/offered them tea
   He began to smile

   (b) He was normally unsociable/couldn't cope with visitors
   He didn't normally show any emotion

10. (I examined my cousin)
    surreptitiously

11. **In your own words**
    He was not at all like/he was totally unlike his mother

12. He was inquisitive/nosey/taking in everything

13. **In your own words**
    He found her intriguing/enthralling/<u>very</u> interesting (must have intensity)

14. They were exaggerated/boastful OR the aunt was showing off/trying to impress/trying to belittle the mother
    Either

15. **In your own words**
    They felt they had to/it was their duty because they were family/relatives
    They wanted to see what they were like

16. Canary suit v tweed suit
    Theatrical   v staid/prim
    Glamorous   v plain
    Any two

17. They were putting on an act/still not at ease

18. Answers can refer to TONE (to make it more conversational/humorous) OR to NARRATIVE VOICE (to give "asides"/introduce adult reflection)

19. Answers should describe CHANGE:
    eg from being "utterly fascinated" to being "ill at ease with"
    OR from being besotted to becoming suspicious
    OR from positive to negative
    AND provide appropriate textual support

English General Level
Reading 2002

1. He was unemployed

2. | whirl | | swish |

   Accept "slamming" also

3. (a) She seems high up/is seated on the edge because she is young/small

   (b) (i) She gravely answered her father

   (ii) She was blowing on each spoonful making a show of it/as she had been taught

4. Because the man was interested/intended to apply/had been out of work for a year like the man in the advert/was attracted by the rewards

   Any two

5. Encouraging his daughter to talk

   OR

   the lively conversation

   OR

   listening to her talk/chatter

6. | | *Paragraph 4* | *Paragraph 5* |
   |---|---|---|
   | To elaborate on an idea | ✔ | |
   | To introduce an explanation | | ✔ |

7. | gushed/fretted | | urgent/commanded |

   Any two

8. He describes the girls face as "prey" as if the air was attacking her

9. (a) Because they do it/repeat it/go through the same process every time/every day

   OR

   Because the father values it as a ceremony

   (b) (. . . in an) accustomed (way . . .)

10. She would feel uncomfortable **OR** affronted to be seen by her friends
    [Also accept reference to the consequences of being seen eg "because they would tease her"]

11. (a) It was organised/business-like/word-processed
    Any one

    (b) (i) Information about school education + appropriate reason (eg lots of experience since then)

    (ii) Requests for referee + appropriate reason (eg they're not likely to say anything bad)

12. (a) He realised that he'd folded the contents wrongly

    OR

    He'd folded the contents wrongly and wanted to change it

    (b) (The word) "Gingerly" is placed at the start of the sentence

    (c) (i) . . . briskly (typed) . . .

    (ii) . . . laborious/two fingered (style) . . .

13. It was a busy place/had a working atmosphere which made it seem a better/luckier place to post it
    [Accept also a negative response based on the idea that the one in his street was unlucky]

14. There were so many (others) that his would be lost/had no hope

15. Answers should deal with the idea that "sideline" = left out/excluded etc

    AND

    that "face in a crowd" = anonymity/one of many/lost/unimportant etc
    [Accept also an appropriate, evaluative generalised comment relating to the effectiveness of the image]

16. (a) He keeps out of sight of her friends/ plays with her/makes her laugh/ talks to her/asks about her morning

    Any two

    (b) Examples include: at breakfast—asking her if it's all right/enjoying or encouraging her chatter/checking she's wrapped up properly/ensuring she's with friends at school (before he leaves)/the idea that without her he wouldn't have the will to keep trying

    (Any two appropriate references, lifts or glosses)

17. Either is acceptable (no mark for choice alone).
    Hope/optimism—the man keeps on trying/shows a professional approach to applying for jobs/is spurred on by his daughter etc.
    Despair, pessimism—he's been out of work for a year/no luck with applications so far/feels the application process is just "wee games"/thinks he's got as little chance as winning a raffle or the pools/feels really left out etc

    (Any two appropriate references for one mark each)

English Credit Level
Reading 2002

1. (i) Blend in/become invisible

    (ii) and be observant
         Reference to spy

2. (a) (i) They wore clothing that was too
              big/loose and could (easily) hide things
              in it

         (ii) Their overcoats/briefcases
              were good for hiding things

    (b) To show the variety/wide range
         of (potential) shoplifters
         Accept also: "to show it's not just young
         people/to show that anyone could be a
         shoplifter"

3. There were lots of them
    they spread (quickly/widely)
    and they were unwanted/a nuisance
    Any two

4. He picked up a wire basket
    pretended to be a shopper
    took an interest in the produce
    Any two

5. Possibilities include:
    sentence structure—long/punctuated as
       succession of phrases (list)
    word-choice—use of verbs
    imagery—public described as an entity

    Also accept reference to deliberate use of "all over
    the shop" in BOTH literal and metaphorical
    senses

6. (a) Holding/touching/"thumbing" the avocados

    (b) (There was) something in her movements
         that was very tense

7. He pretended to be a (puzzled) man looking for
    his wife/a man who'd lost his wife

8. (i) Use of: a/an/one/individual/solitary
         Any two
         [Accept also appropriate generalised
         statement]

    (ii) Each item is given a sentence **on its own**

9. (a) Both pay for/declare something
         in the hope of getting away with stolen/more
         valuable goods

    (b) An amateur tactic
         OR
         It was easy . . . conscience/. . . who wanted
         to be caught

10. Because you find out that he had guessed
    correctly
    about her stealing (the packets of seeds)

11. Surprised—you don't expect a shoplifter to want
    to be arrested
    Intrigued—you want to know why she said
    "Before I do something worse"
    Not surprised—the woman had already shown
    signs of odd behaviour
    Sympathetic—she looked upset/distressed
    eg shaking visibly/tears loomed
    Note: answers to "Not surprised" or
    "sympathetic" may refer to appropriate evidence
    from earlier in the passage
    Any one justified by close reference to the text.

12. (i) He wondered if people would think that
         they were a couple shopping

    (ii) He avoided going through the office area/
         went up the back stairs
         so she would not be seen/embarassed

13. Reference to any TWO of: very small table/only
    one chair/which is an upright one/the window is
    barred (like a cell—possibly dark)/the only
    outlook is the fire escape/wall-mounted telephone

14. . . . as if her head might explode./It ripped out
    of her . . . prisoner for years.
    Either + appropriate comment on intensity of
    image.

15. He says: " . . . it was just absent-mindedness."/
    "You intended to pay for these."

16. Because the pictures on the packets remind her of
    her husband/his garden

17. Each emotion should be linked to an appropriate
    reference or comment—eg he was always in the
    garden/the garden is now abandoned/her husband
    is dead/she is experiencing financial hardship

18. Either is acceptable:
    —let her go—sympathy established + appropriate
    reference
    —charge her—concern for his job + appropriate
    reference

19. The woman's husband—he was never around,
    always in his garden/(although dead) still affects
    her life
    OR
    Imaginary—the "invisible man" who shakes
    woman violently

English General Level
Reading 2003

1. (i) reference to 'creaked'/word choice
    (ii) reference to short sentence/sentence structure

2. weak/about to go out/flame moving (from side to side) AND eerie/scary atmosphere

3. ironic
    comment, e.g. they were afraid + reference, e.g. running away/went white

4. teasing/tormenting etc

5. (i) reference to Victorian (novelist)
    (ii) reference to carriage

6. to provide additional information/detail/parenthesis

7. uses a list
    uses horrific/dramatic images
    uses/refers to colours
    uses/refers to blood dripping/pointed fangs/wolves, skulls and skeletons/human victims
    gives a powerful description of Dracula
    Any two

8. adds humour/makes reader laugh/to make passage less frightening/less serious/relieves the tension
    Any one

9. to find out/see
    if it was too scary/frightening/if it was suitable for the boys

10. (One vampire hand was) "quite enough"

11. disapproving/thinks they are very touristy/rubbish
    Any one

12. magnificent/thinks it is very beautiful/very attractive
    Any one

13. being ironic/to show that it is not really a castle

14. (Prince) Vlad Tepes

15. Any two from:
    brings people (to Romania)
    in large numbers
    reference to economic benefits

16. exterior: cold/unwelcoming/"dramatic"
    interior: warm/"welcoming"/"cosy"

17. he had a simple costume/paper fangs/jumped around corners/jumped down steps/connotations of play/doing these things on a sunny August day/had wooden daggers/he was only a child
    Any two

18. powerful/strong/burning sensation
    made up of many/various ingredients

19. (a) How: scared/frightened/afraid
        Why: because of all of the dead animals on display/or an example of the animals on display
    (b) "(Once the children) got over the fear"
        "feasted (on thick stew)"

20. hiking
    camping

21. (a) concerned/worried/anxious/upset
    (b) looking forward to making money
        worried it will spoil the town/things will never be the same again
        (Generalised answer, e.g. some for, some against = 1)
    (c) link to heading/beginning of the passage
        humour/show Dracula's disapproval/to show Dracula would agree with her
        (Literal interpretation: association with vampires and undead/still moving = 1)

22. reference to the pun "a big stake"
    reference to summarises the passage

English Credit Level
Reading 2003

1. introduces the topic/subject of the passage
   makes an impact/catches the reader's attention

2. part of a (well known) saying (dead as the dodo)
   because of its sound

3. it contradicts itself
   (as) a myth is something that has never existed
   the dodo did exist/is not a myth
   Any two

4. (i) "bizarre"
   (ii) "enigma"

5. image of Victorian gentleman
   which makes it ridiculous/exaggerated
   lift or gloss of "real" to "surreal"

6. something awful/dramatic was going to happen/it
   was going to have tragic consequences/it was going
   to result in death/it was going to be unlucky
   Any one

7. it acts as an introduction to/link with what follows
   OR it emphasises the strangeness of the bird

8. it appeared/seemed/looked
   as if it would not work/as if it would not be of any
   use

9. allows him to explore/suggest/consider/offer/
   introduce possible explanations
   AND reference to reader involvement

10. reference to Dutch artists putting them in
    (fashionable) paintings/
    sent to Europe/
    exhibited
    Any three
    (Any two = 1; any 1 = 0)

11. convey the idea of detection/investigation/tracking/
    hard to find

12. only the best survive/if it is useless it won't
    survive/
    gloss of "poorly designed and hapless creatures"
    e.g. not built for survival/to survive/not intelligent
    enough to survive

13. "misrepresented"

14. (i) fat v lean/fat v sinuous neck
    (ii) low down v standing up/squat v upright

15. to show/illustrate/emphasise
    lots of things to be answered **OR**
    how little we know

16. "stuffed"
    reference to unsuccessful attempt to preserve the
    dodo

17. it was the closest
    large piece of land/continent

18. conveys the idea of travelling from island to island
    conveys the idea of short journeys between islands,
    humour
    comparison to modern tourists/back-packers
    Any two

19. (i) "believes"
    (ii) "possibly"

20. (i) it was "terrible to eat"/they called it a
        "nauseating fowl"/it tasted awful
    (ii) no bones were discovered in the household
         rubbish

21. upset breeding
    destroyed eggs
    fought for food
    (Any two = 1; any 1 = 0)

22. seemed harmless
    but in fact it was damaging/harmful

23. it conveys/emphasises the speed/short time
    in which the dodo became extinct/was completely
    destroyed

24. interviews with/reference to experts/scientists/
    doctors/archaeologists/museums, zoological detail/
    historical context/dates etc
    + appropriate comment

25. what the dodo really looked like
    why the dodo really died out

English General Level
Reading 2004

1. encouraged OR embarrassing

2. associated it with red flowers which they associated with nectar/food

3. suggests no proof/doubt

4. Both:
   - Beatty's Guest Ranch
   - (in the mountains of) South-East Arizona/Mexico border

5. One of:
   - Expression/term used by hummingbird watchers
   - That is what hummingbird watchers call them
   - It is a colloquialism/nickname/slang

6. Any one from: (including explanation)
   - **Use of list** - gives number/range of feederlocations.
   - **Inversion** - links, develops information from previous sentence.
   - **Parenthesis** - gives additional information.

7. mind-boggling

8. great speed
   AND
   moving in all directions/chaotically

9. (hovering with) immaculate precision
   OR
   experienced helicopter pilots
   OR
   both/complete expression

10. Any two from:
    - So many varieties
    - Speed of the movement
    - Constant changes of colour

11. One of:
    - He believes their behaviour is trivial/unimportant.
    - He thinks they are childish.
    - He thinks it is petty.

12. (i) attraction/to show off

    (ii) survival/camouflage

13. The (different) **sound** of their **wings**.

14. Allusion to proverb
    OR
    Shows closeness to the bird AND makes use of alliteration

15. Any two from:
    - Contrasting **small** and **large**
    - Contrasting **stationary** and **moving**
    - Contrasting **delicate** and **clumsy**

16. One of:
    - He was **amazed**
    - He felt it was **incredible**
    - He was **privileged**
    - It was **beyond his expectations**

17. Both:
    - A hummingbird (constantly) needs lots of food/nectar.
    - Like a fast car - needs lots of fuel OR like a busy person - needs lots of food/energy.

18. Both:
    - Fierce/aggressive
    - Competitive/territorial

19. Need both to **identify** and **comment**. e.g.
    - **Structure**: the position of "Dutifully" at the beginning of the sentence to emphasise he is following instructions/to emphasise his reluctance.
    OR
    - **Punctuation**: the use of dots to suggest a pause
    OR
    - **Punctuation**: reference to list/commas to highlight number/sequence of actions.

20. (sat there for) an eternity.

21. unexpected / had not expected it / taken aback / surprised

22. Need both a valid **reference/example** and an **appropriate comment**.
    e.g. "A dress and high heels are optional" – a self-deprecating aside included solely to create a ridiculous image of the (male) writer in female clothing.

23. Need both an **appropriate viewpoint/feeling** and a **quotation/reference**.
    e.g. He was amazed and touched by it. "every bit as impressive as rubbing shoulders with mountain gorillas".

English Credit Level
Reading 2004

1. (i) "Abruptly"

    (ii) "seized"

2. Either or both:
    - "worse than the brigands (of childhood tales)"
    - "a most horrible and wild stranger"

3. not moving/no movement
    AND
    except for/only his hands

4. (i) insanity/madness

    (ii) at being alone

5. Both:
    - Hair falling over his face.
    - Bushy/large/out of control beard.

6. They were old wounds/they had been bleeding
    AND
    They were now reopened/still bleeding/not healed/new

7. (i) **List/repetition** (of phrases) + Explanation: e.g. reference to cumulative effect/variety of smells/climactic effect

    (ii) **Word choice**: inconceivably foul/reek of rotting flesh/festering wounds/ancient perspiration + Explanation. e.g. words which detail vividly the unpleasantness.

8. (*a*) fear, sympathy

    (*b*) The use of the question/the writer gets Pelagia to ask herself a question

9. Get rid of him/get him to go away/come back next day

10. Any two from:
    - Reference to what he says makes no sense
    - Responds inappropriately
    - Confused
    - Repeats "ice"

11. Any two from:
    - Sharpness
    - Noise
    - Faces/people

12. Any two from:
    - Use of repetition
    - Onomatopoeia
    - Short sentences
    - List
    - Personification

13. Both:
    - Go for/seek help
    - Guard/take care of the house

14. (i) Only

    (ii) discarded

15. One of:
    - He is **disappointed**.
    - He is **angry**.
    - He is **annoyed**.
    - He is **sad**.

16. List of/series of/lots of follow on questions.

17. Either:
    - Desperate to get to her but now holds her at arms length
    OR
    - She wouldn't have wanted to touch him anyway because of his appearance or smell

18. Fiancé ✓
    Justification: any reference to "betrothed"/"loved and desired and missed"

19. Reference to any one of:
    - repetition of "accusation"
    - "rankled"
    - the metaphor
    - "angry resentful monster"
    - "from the moment of his departure"
    - "first thing"

20. She was more astonished/surprised/shocked/disgusted than she was by his dirt/filth.

21. **Pelagia** – e.g. frightened initially, then angry. (Clear change must be indicated.)

    Mandras – quiet/motionless/disorientated, then more assertive/active/clear thinking. (Clear change must be indicated.)

22. Answer must show:
    - An opinion
    - Adequate explanation
    - Supporting textual reference or quotation
      e.g. Mandras, because he has obviously suffered a terrible ordeal and is in need of medical help and care. "his feet were bound with bandages that were both caked with old congealed blood, and the bright stains of fresh."

English General Level Reading 2005

1. 6 years of (yellowing) newspapers
   70 videos of their performances

2. (i) She has spent £3,000

   (ii) She has seen them 17 times

   (iii) She now thinks/believes the band recognises her (as an acquaintance if not a friend)

3. It suggests she targets/singles him out/she is focused

4. She isn't really (an acquaintance))/being ironic

5. • Reference to her anger/strength of feeling.
   • Reference to <u>having to</u> defend him

6. Surprised/Disapproving

7. (a) Relaxed

   (b) she freely admits/has never caused me problems/sees nothing odd in it/I am not missing out on anything

8. (i) "about a third of people suffer (from 'celebrity worship syndrome')" Gloss or quote

   (ii) "may affect our mood" Gloss or quote

   (iii) "affects their mental well-being" Gloss or quote

9. To involve the reader/make you think/introduce the debate/introduce the central idea of the passage

10. Alexander the Great

11. (cultural phenomenon) for centuries/more than 2,000 years ago

12. • Some attempt to gloss: "hundreds of star images"
    • Some attempt to gloss some or all of "advertising . . . other forms" eg mass media etc

13. cannot get enough/shows their need/desire/strength/intensity of feeling/addiction to etc

14. To prove how famous David Beckham is
    OR To highlight the extent of celebrity culture
    OR For humour + suitable comment

15. The internet

16. • Some attempt to gloss "gauge personality" eg what kind of person
    • Some attempt to gloss "level of interest in celebrities" eg how interested you are in famous people

17. (i) It exists in America & UK

    (ii) They have plastic surgery/he gives an example of a person who has become Pierce Brosnan

18. To show/indicate/highlight/emphasise a change/the opposite argument/the good side

19. (fables once sought in) fairytales

20. They were first/leaders in their field

21. • Attempt to gloss "dietary regime" eg improve diet
    • Reference to being fitter/healthier/better at football/having improved attitude/commitment to football or sport in general

22. (a) feel good/better about yourself ie gloss of "raising their self-esteem

    (b) They are respected and highly regarded.

23. • Full explanation of the metaphor
    • Sums up passage
    • negative connotation/effect of celebrity worship

English Credit Level
Reading 2005

1. Both are a hundred years old

2. To suggest the length of the railway

3. epitome

4. • sums up
   • idea of European Cairo/contrasts within the city
   • alliterative quality/catchy

5. • use of the list
   • reference to high ranking people

6. (i) riotous (send offs and welcomes)

   (ii) escaped an assassination attempt (at Cairo Station on his return)

7. Not about anyone important/about an ordinary person

8. bliss

9. Any two of
   • lots of cars v few cars
   • bright v dark
   • lots of buildings v few buildings
   • large v small buildings
   • ordinary appearance v extraordinary appearance of men
   • lots of people v few people

10. • "troop" suggests idea of formation/order/purpose
    • "sorcerers" suggests magical/scary appearance.
    • sums up the previous idea
    negative comments acceptable if fully explained

11. Any two of
    • (long) mild face
    • but what's the use in fussing
    • a very gentle man/doesn't say much in the morning/says "Durn"

12. woke occasionally/spent most of the time asleep looking at the countryside/surroundings

13. (a) to suggest a sense of wonderment/realisation/awe at the enormity

    (b) it is what the sign says/a quote

14. Any two of
    • reference to exotic location
    • colourful
    • stress-free lifestyle
    • old fashioned
    • rural
    • idea of abundance

15. (a) what he had seen of the past in museums he sees now before his eyes/is still there

    (b) same food
    same cooking utensils

16. faffing
    comment eg informal/colloquial/contemporary

17. (a) It is fertile and tranquil.

    (b) fertile – green fields/plots/dates/plantations
    tranquil – slow moving/clouds on surface/hawks drifting/river feluccas with sails

18. Any two of
    • shape/full of air/movement/
    • colour/size

19. (a) suggests a sense of arrival/satisfaction/climax/expectation/excitement/anticipation

    (b) use of short sentence
    through word order/inversion

20. politics/architecture/museums/tombs/artefacts
    Any two references
    OR Any one reference + appropriate comment

    people/culture/landscape/food details/method(s) of travel
    Any two references
    OR Any one reference + appropriate comment